easy cupcakes

D0550089

easy cupcakes

100 fuss-free recipes for everyday cooking

MARKS &
SPENCER

Marks and Spencer p.l.c.
PO Box 3339
Chester CH99 9QS

shop online
www.marksandspencer.com

Copyright © Exclusive Editions Publishing Ltd 2011

ISBN: 978-1-84960-746-9

Printed in China

Introduction by Linda Doeser
New recipes by Angela Drake
Cover photo is cupcake © Digital Vision/Getty Images
Additional photography by Clive Streeter
Additional food styling by Angela Drake and Teresa Goldfinch

The views expressed in this book are those of the author but they
are general views only and readers are urged to consult a relevant
and qualified specialist for individual advice in particular situations.
Marks and Spencer p.l.c. and Exclusive Editions Limited hereby
exclude all liability to the extent permitted by law for any errors
or omissions in this book and for any loss, damage or expense
(whether direct or indirect) suffered by a third party relying on any
information contained in this book.

Notes for the Reader
This book uses both metric and imperial measurements. Follow
the same units of measurement throughout; do not mix metric and
imperial. All spoon measurements are level: teaspoons are assumed
to be 5 ml, and tablespoons are assumed to be 15 ml. Unless
otherwise stated, milk is assumed to be full fat, eggs and individual
vegetables are medium, and pepper is freshly ground black pepper.

The times given are an approximate guide only. Preparation times
differ according to the techniques used by different people and the
cooking times may also vary from those given. Optional ingredients,
variations or serving suggestions have not been included in the
calculations.

Recipes using raw or very lightly cooked eggs should be avoided
by infants, the elderly, pregnant women, convalescents and anyone
suffering from an illness. Pregnant and breastfeeding women are
advised to avoid eating peanuts and peanut products. Sufferers
from nut allergies should be aware that some of the ready-made
ingredients used in the recipes in this book may contain nuts.
Always check the packaging before use.

Contents

Introduction

Two, maybe even three generations have happy childhood memories of birthday party tables spread with all manner of exciting goodies but almost always featuring a colourful display of iced cupcakes decorated with sugar sprinkles, glacé cherries or chocolate buttons. However, in the last few years, cupcakes have undergone a revolutionary change. While still beloved by children, they have entered a new era of popularity with adults – and not just as a result of nostalgia. Busy people on their morning rush to the office are now just as likely to buy a cupcake with their latte as a muffin. With all kinds of new recipes, incorporating a wide range of ingredients and flavours, and far more sophisticated decoration than simple glacé or buttercream icing, the cupcake has come of age.

That said, they remain just as quick and easy to make at home. Whether made with traditional ingredients and flavourings, such as sultanas or cocoa powder, or something more unusual, such as polenta or saffron, the basic technique is unchanged. It's simply a matter of whisking the ingredients together to make a light sponge cake mixture that will rise when baked in a medium–hot oven. Even the most inexperienced cook can whisk up a batch of cupcakes in a matter of minutes. In fact, these days when most kitchens have electric mixers, making cupcakes is virtually effortless.

Cupcakes don't have to be decorated, especially if they contain delicious extra flavourings such as spices, chocolate chips, nuts or fresh or dried fruit. Risen and golden brown in their neat little paper cases, they are still very tempting. However, decorating them does provide an opportunity to explore your creative side. Simple drizzled icings and ready-made sugar and chocolate shapes, as well as all sorts of sweets, remain popular, but many other ingredients, from stem ginger to whipped cream and from cream cheese to flower petals, are just as easy. You can also decorate cupcakes for a special occasion such as Christmas, Easter or Halloween, or for birthdays or baby showers. Many of the suggestions in this book are ideal for adults who may not have quite such a sweet tooth as children.

Like all kinds of cooking, but especially baking, when making cupcakes there are some dos and a few don'ts. It is worth reading through the tips on the opposite page to avoid disappointment and to guarantee success.

Top Tips for Success

• Always read through the recipe before you start and check that you have all the ingredients required.

• Do not substitute plain for self-raising flour (or vice versa) — they are not interchangeable. However, if you have run out of self-raising flour, you can use plain flour if you mix baking powder with it — add 4 teaspoons baking powder to every 500 g/1 lb 2 oz plain flour.

• Remove ingredients stored in the refrigerator 30 minutes before using to allow them to come to room temperature. This is especially important with eggs which may curdle when added to the mixture if they are very cold. Butter should also be at room temperature, as if it is very soft or even melted, it will spoil the texture of the cakes.

• Measure ingredients carefully — this is more important in baking than in almost any other kind of cooking. Spoon measurements should be levelled off with the blade of a knife. To avoid overfilling and spoiling the flavour of your cakes, do not hold the measuring spoon over the mixing bowl when pouring small quantities of liquid such as vanilla extract. The jug for measuring larger amounts of liquid

should stand on a flat surface and you should check the measure at eye level.

• Using an electric mixer is quick and easy, but be careful not to overbeat the mixture. A wooden spoon works just as well but requires a little more time and effort.

• Once you have mixed the cake batter, do not leave it standing for any length of time, but spoon it immediately into the paper cases and bake, otherwise your cakes may be flat.

• Do not overfill the paper cases or the mixture will bubble over during cooking, creating misshapen cakes and a nasty mess in the oven.

• Always preheat the oven to the specified temperature, otherwise the cakes may not rise evenly or at all.

• Bake the cakes on a shelf towards the top of a conventional oven. If they are too high, the tops may become brown before the insides are cooked through. If they are too low, they will take too long to cook and will dry out. The temperature in fan-assisted ovens is even throughout.

• Transfer baked cupcakes, still in their paper cases, to a wire rack and leave to cool completely before decorating, unless the recipe specifies otherwise.

1

Gorgeous Cupcakes

vanilla-frosted cupcakes

MAKES 12
115 g/4 oz butter, softened
115 g/4 oz caster sugar
2 eggs, lightly beaten
115 g/4 oz self-raising flour
1 tbsp milk
1 tbsp hundreds and thousands

frosting
175 g/6 oz unsalted butter, softened
1 tsp vanilla extract
280 g/10 oz icing sugar, sifted

1 Preheat the oven to 180°C/350°F/Gas Mark 4. Put 12 paper baking cases in a bun tray or put 12 double-layer paper cases on a baking tray.

2 Put the butter and sugar in a bowl and beat together until light and fluffy. Gradually beat in the eggs. Sift in the flour and, using a metal spoon, fold into the mixture with the milk. Spoon the mixture into the paper cases.

3 Bake the cupcakes in the preheated oven for 20 minutes or until golden brown and firm to the touch. Transfer to a wire rack and leave to cool.

4 To make the frosting, put the butter and vanilla extract in a bowl and, using an electric hand whisk, beat until the butter is pale and very soft. Gradually add the icing sugar, whisking well after each addition. Spoon the frosting into a large piping bag fitted with a medium star-shaped nozzle and pipe large swirls of frosting on the top of each cupcake. Sprinkle with hundreds and thousands.

fairy cupcakes

MAKES 16

115 g/4 oz unsalted butter

115 g/4 oz caster sugar

2 eggs, beaten

115 g/4 oz self-raising flour, sifted

sugar flowers, hundreds and thousands, glacé cherries, and/or chocolate strands, to decorate

icing

200 g/7 oz icing sugar

about 2 tbsp warm water

a few drops of food colouring (optional)

1 Preheat the oven to 190°C/375°F/Gas Mark 5. Put 16 paper baking cases in 2 bun trays or put 16 double-layer paper cases on a baking tray.

2 Place the butter and caster sugar in a large bowl and cream together with a wooden spoon or electric hand whisk until pale and fluffy.

3 Gradually add the eggs, beating well after each addition. Fold in the flour lightly and evenly using a metal spoon. Spoon the mixture into the paper cases and bake in the preheated oven for 15–20 minutes. Cool on a wire rack.

4 For the icing, sift the icing sugar into a bowl and stir in just enough water to mix to a smooth paste that is thick enough to coat the back of a wooden spoon. Stir in a few drops of food colouring, if using, then spread the icing over the fairy cakes and decorate as desired.

mini sweetie cupcakes

MAKES 18

55 g/2 oz self-raising flour

¼ tsp baking powder

55 g/2 oz soft tub margarine

55 g/2 oz caster sugar

1 egg, lightly beaten

sweets, to decorate

icing

85 g/3 oz icing sugar

2–3 tsp water

1 Preheat the oven to 180°C/350°F/Gas Mark 4. Put 18 paper mini paper cases on a baking tray.

2 Sift the flour and baking powder into a bowl. Add the margarine, sugar and egg and, using an electric hand whisk, beat together until smooth. Spoon the mixture into the paper cases.

3 Bake the cupcakes in the preheated oven for 15–20 minutes until risen and golden brown. Transfer to a wire rack and leave to cool.

4 To make the icing, sift the icing sugar into a bowl and beat in the water to make a smooth thick icing. Spoon a little icing in the centre of each cupcake and decorate each with a sweet. Leave to set.

rose petal cupcakes

MAKES 12

115 g/4 oz butter, softened

115 g/4 oz caster sugar

2 eggs, lightly beaten

1 tbsp milk

few drops of essence of rose oil

¼ tsp vanilla extract

175 g/6 oz self-raising flour, sifted

crystallized rose petals, to decorate

frosting

85 g/3 oz butter, softened

175 g/6 oz icing sugar

pink food colouring (optional)

1 Preheat the oven to 200°C/400°F/Gas Mark 6. Put 12 paper baking cases in a bun tray, or put 12 double-layer paper cases on a baking tray.

2 Put the butter and sugar in a bowl and beat together until light and fluffy. Gradually add the eggs, beating well after each addition. Stir in the milk, rose oil and vanilla extract then, using a metal spoon, fold in the flour. Spoon the mixture into the paper cases and bake the cupcakes in the preheated oven for 12–15 minutes until well risen and golden brown. Transfer to a wire rack and leave to cool.

3 To make the frosting, put the butter in a large bowl and beat until fluffy. Sift in the icing sugar and mix well together. If wished, add a few drops of pink food colouring to complement the rose petals.

4 When the cupcakes are cold, put a blob of frosting on top of each cake. Top with 1–2 crystallized rose petals to decorate.

pink & white cupcakes

MAKES 16

115 g/4 oz self-raising flour
1 tsp baking powder
115 g/4 oz butter, softened
115 g/4 oz caster sugar
2 eggs, lightly beaten
1 tbsp milk
few drops red food colouring

topping
1 egg white
175 g/6 oz caster sugar
2 tbsp hot water
large pinch of cream of tartar
2 tbsp raspberry jam
3 tbsp desiccated coconut, lightly toasted

1 Preheat the oven to 180°C/350°F/Gas Mark 4. Put 16 paper baking cases in 2 bun trays or put 16 double-layer paper cases on a large baking tray.

2 Sift the flour and baking powder into a bowl. Add the butter, sugar and eggs and, using an electric hand whisk, beat together until smooth. Mix together the milk and food colouring and whisk into the mixture until evenly blended. Spoon the mixture into the paper cases.

3 Bake the cupcakes in the preheated oven for 20 minutes or until risen and golden brown. Transfer to a wire rack and leave to cool.

4 To make the topping, put the egg white, sugar, water and cream of tartar in a heatproof bowl set over a saucepan of simmering water. Using an electric hand whisk, beat for 5–6 minutes until the mixture is thick and softly peaks when the whisk is lifted.

5 Spread a layer of raspberry jam over each cupcake then swirl over the frosting. Sprinkle with the toasted coconut.

lemon polenta cupcakes

MAKES 14

115 g/4 oz butter, softened

115 g/ 4 oz golden caster sugar

finely grated rind and juice of ½ lemon

2 eggs, lightly beaten

55 g/2 oz plain flour

1 tsp baking powder

55 g/2 oz quick-cook polenta

crystallized violets, to decorate

frosting

150 g/5½ oz mascarpone cheese

2 tsp finely grated lemon rind

25 g/1 oz icing sugar, sifted

1 Preheat the oven to 180°C/350°F/Gas Mark 4. Put 14 paper baking cases in 2 bun trays or put 14 double-layer paper cases on a baking tray.

2 Put the butter and sugar in a bowl and beat together until light and fluffy. Beat in the lemon rind and juice. Gradually beat in the eggs. Sift in the flour and baking powder and, using a metal spoon, fold gently into the mixture with the polenta. Spoon the mixture into the paper cases.

3 Bake the cupcakes in the preheated oven for 20 minutes or golden brown and firm to the touch. Transfer to a wire rack and leave to cool.

4 To make the frosting, beat the mascarpone cheese until smooth then beat in the lemon rind and icing sugar. Spread the frosting over the cupcakes. Store the cupcakes in the refrigerator until ready to serve. Decorate each cupcake with a crystallized violet just before serving

iced madeira cupcakes

MAKES 16

115 g/4 oz butter, softened

115 g/4 oz golden caster sugar

finely grated rind of ½ lemon

2 large eggs, lightly beaten

175 g/6 oz self-raising flour

40 g/1½ oz ground almonds

55 g/2 oz candied citron peel, thinly sliced

icing

55 g/2 oz icing sugar

3 tsp warm water

1 Preheat the oven to 180°C/350°F/Gas Mark 4. Put 16 paper baking cases in 2 bun trays or put 16 double-layer paper cases on a baking tray.

2 Put the butter, sugar and lemon rind in a bowl and beat together until light and fluffy. Gradually beat in the eggs. Sift in the flour and, using a metal spoon, fold gently into the mixture with the ground almonds. Spoon the mixture into the paper cases. Put a slice of citron peel on the top of each cupcake.

3 Bake the cupcakes in the preheated oven for 20–25 minutes or until risen and golden brown. Transfer to a wire rack and leave to cool.

4 To make the icing, sift the icing sugar into a bowl and add enough of the warm water to make a runny icing. Using a pastry brush, glaze the top of each cupcake with the icing. Leave to set.

poppy seed & orange cupcakes

MAKES 12

2 tbsp poppy seeds, plus extra to decorate

2 tbsp hot milk

85 g/3 oz butter, softened

85 g/3 oz caster sugar

finely grated rind of ½ orange

1 large egg, lightly beaten

100 g/3½ oz self-raising flour

frosting

85 g/3 oz butter, softened

finely grated rind of ½ orange

175 g/6 oz icing sugar, sifted

1–2 tbsp orange juice

1 Preheat the oven to 180°C/350°F/Gas Mark 4. Put 12 paper baking cases in a bun tray or put 12 double-layer paper cases on a baking tray. Place the poppy seeds and milk in a small bowl and set aside for 10 minutes.

2 Put the butter, sugar and orange rind in a bowl and beat together until light and fluffy. Gradually beat in the egg. Sift in the flour and, using a metal spoon, fold gently into the mixture with the poppy seeds and milk. Spoon the mixture into the paper cases.

3 Bake the cupcakes in the preheated oven for 20 minutes or until risen and golden brown. Transfer to a wire rack and leave to cool.

4 To make the frosting, put the butter and orange rind in a bowl and beat until fluffy. Gradually beat in the icing sugar and enough orange juice to make a smooth and creamy frosting. Put the icing in a piping bag, fitted with a large star nozzle. When the cupcakes are cold, pipe a swirl on top of each cupcake and decorate with the poppy seeds.

warm strawberry cupcakes

MAKES 6

115 g/4 oz butter, softened, plus extra for greasing

4 tbsp strawberry jam

115 g/4 oz caster sugar

2 eggs, lightly beaten

1 tsp vanilla extract

115 g/4 oz self-raising flour

small whole fresh strawberries, to decorate

icing sugar, for dusting

1 Preheat the oven to 180°C/350°F/Gas Mark 4. Grease six 200-ml/7-fl oz heavy round teacups with butter. Spoon 2 teaspoons of the strawberry jam in the bottom of each teacup.

2 Put the butter and sugar in a bowl and beat together until light and fluffy. Gradually add the eggs, beating well after each addition, then add the vanilla extract. Sift in the flour and, using a large metal spoon, fold it into the mixture. Spoon the mixture into the teacups.

3 Stand the cups in a roasting tin, then pour in enough hot water to come one third up the sides of the cups. Bake the cupcakes in the preheated oven for 40 minutes, or until well risen and golden brown, and a skewer, inserted in the centre, comes out clean. If over-browning, cover the cupcakes with a sheet of foil. Leave the cupcakes to cool for 2–3 minutes, then carefully lift the cups from the tin and place them on saucers.

4 Scatter a few of the whole strawberries over the cakes, then dust them with sifted icing sugar. Serve warm.

caramel cupcakes

MAKES 12

85 g/3 oz butter, softened

55 g/2 oz soft dark brown sugar

1 tbsp golden syrup

1 large egg, lightly beaten

100 g/3½ oz self-raising flour

1 tsp grated nutmeg

2 tbsp milk

topping

115 g/4 oz soft light brown sugar

1 small egg white

1 tbsp hot water

pinch of cream of tartar

1 Preheat the oven to 180°C/350°F/Gas Mark 4. Put 12 paper baking cases in a bun tray or put 12 double-layer paper cases on a baking tray.

2 Put the butter, sugar and golden syrup in a bowl and beat together until light and fluffy. Gradually beat in the egg. Sift in the flour and, using a metal spoon, fold gently into the mixture with the nutmeg and milk. Spoon the mixture into the paper cases.

3 Bake the cupcakes in the preheated oven for 15–20 minutes or until risen and golden brown. Transfer to a wire rack and leave to cool.

4 To make the topping, put all the ingredients in a heatproof bowl set over a saucepan of simmering water. Using an electric hand whisk beat for 5–6 minutes until the mixture is thick and softly peaking when the whisk is lifted. Swirl the topping over the cupcakes.

butterscotch cupcakes

MAKES 28

175 g/6 oz plain white flour

1 tbsp baking powder

175 g/6 oz unsalted butter, softened

175 g/6 oz light muscovado sugar

3 eggs, beaten

1 tsp vanilla extract

topping

2 tbsp golden syrup

25 g/1 oz unsalted butter

2 tbsp light muscovado sugar

1 Preheat the oven to 190°C/375°F/Gas Mark 5. Place 28 paper cases into bun tins or put 28 double-layer paper cases onto baking trays.

2 Sift the flour and baking powder into a large bowl and add the butter, sugar, eggs and vanilla extract. Beat well until the mixture is smooth.

3 Divide the mixture between the paper cases. Bake in the preheated oven for 15–20 minutes, or until risen, firm and golden brown. Transfer the cupcakes to a wire rack to cool.

4 For the topping, place the golden syrup, butter and sugar in a small pan and heat gently, stirring, until the sugar dissolves. Bring to the boil and cook, stirring, for about 1 minute. Drizzle over the cupcakes and leave to set.

red velvet cupcakes

MAKES 12

140 g/5 oz plain flour

1 tsp bicarbonate of soda

2 tbsp cocoa powder

115 g/4 oz butter, softened

140 g/5 oz caster sugar

1 large egg, beaten

125 ml/4 fl oz buttermilk

1 tsp vanilla extract

1 tbsp red food colouring

red coloured sugar or red sugar sprinkles, to decorate

frosting

140 g/5 oz full-fat soft cheese

85 g/3 oz unsalted butter, softened

280 g/10 oz icing sugar, sifted

1 Preheat the oven to 180°C/350°F/Gas Mark 4. Put 12 paper baking cases in a bun tray or put 12 double-layer cases on a large baking tray.

2 Sift together the flour, bicarbonate of soda and cocoa powder. Place the butter and sugar in a bowl and beat together until pale and creamy. Gradually beat in the egg and half the flour mixture. Beat in the buttermilk, vanilla extract and food colouring. Fold in the remaining flour mixture. Spoon the mixture into the paper cases.

3 Bake the cupcakes in the preheated oven for 15–20 minutes until risen and firm to the touch. Transfer to a wire rack and leave to cool.

4 To make the frosting, put the soft cheese and butter in a bowl and blend together with a spatula. Beat in the icing sugar until smooth and creamy. Swirl the frosting on the top of the cupcakes. Sprinkle with the red sugar.

fudge & raisin cupcakes

MAKES 10

115 g/4 oz vanilla fudge, cut into small chunks

1 tbsp milk

85 g/3 oz butter, softened

40 g/1½ oz soft light brown sugar

1 large egg, lightly beaten

100 g/3½ oz self-raising flour

25 g/1 oz raisins

1 Preheat the oven to 190°C/375°F/Gas Mark 5. Put 10 paper baking cases in a bun tray or put 10 double-layer paper cases on a baking tray.

2 Put half the fudge in a heatproof bowl with the milk and set over a saucepan of gently simmering water and leave until the fudge has melted. Remove from the heat and stir until smooth. Cool for 10 minutes.

3 Put the butter and sugar into a bowl and beat together until light and fluffy. Gradually beat in the egg. Sift in the flour and, using a metal spoon, fold gently into the mixture with the raisins. Fold in the melted fudge. Spoon the mixture into the paper cases. Scatter the remaining fudge chunks over the cupcakes.

4 Bake the cupcakes in the preheated oven for 15–20 minutes or until risen and golden brown. Transfer to a wire rack and leave to cool.

drizzled honey cupcakes

MAKES 12

85 g/3 oz self-raising flour

¼ tsp ground cinnamon

pinch of ground cloves

pinch of grated nutmeg

85 g/3 oz butter, softened

85 g/3 oz caster sugar

1 tbsp clear honey

finely grated rind of 1 orange

2 eggs, lightly beaten

40 g/1½ oz walnut pieces, finely chopped

topping

15 g/½ oz walnut pieces, finely chopped

¼ tsp ground cinnamon

2 tbsp clear honey

juice of 1 orange

1 Preheat the oven to 190°C/375°F/Gas Mark 5. Put 12 paper baking cases in a bun tray, or put 12 double-layer paper cases on a baking tray.

2 Sift the flour, cinnamon, cloves and nutmeg together into a bowl. Put the butter and sugar in a separate bowl and beat together until light and fluffy. Beat in the honey and orange rind, then gradually add the eggs, beating well after each addition. Using a metal spoon, fold in the flour mixture. Stir in the walnuts, then spoon the mixture into the paper cases.

3 Bake the cupcakes in the preheated oven for 20 minutes, or until well risen and golden brown. Transfer to a wire rack and leave to cool.

4 To make the topping, mix together the walnuts and cinnamon. Put the honey and orange juice in a saucepan and heat gently, stirring, until combined.

5 When the cupcakes have almost cooled, prick the tops all over with a fork or skewer and then drizzle with the warm honey mixture. Sprinkle the walnut mixture over the top of each cupcake and serve warm or cold.

hot marmalade cupcakes

MAKES 4

1 small orange

85 g/3 oz butter, softened, plus extra for greasing

85 g/3 oz caster sugar

1 large egg, lightly beaten

115 g/4 oz self-raising flour, sifted

2 tbsp fine shred marmalade, warmed

crème fraîche, to serve

1 Put the orange in a saucepan and cover with water. Bring to the boil then reduce the heat and cover and simmer for 1 hour until soft. Remove the orange from the water and leave to cool for 30 minutes.

2 Preheat the oven to 180°C/350°F/Gas Mark 4. Grease four 150-ml/5-fl oz ovenproof teacups or dishes (such as ramekins) with butter.

3 Cut the orange in chunks and remove any pips. Put all the orange chunks (rind included) into a food processor and blend until finely minced. Add the butter, sugar, egg and flour and process until well blended. Spoon the mixture into the teacups or dishes.

4 Put the cups or dishes on a baking sheet and bake in the preheated oven for 25–30 minutes or until risen, golden brown and firm to the touch. Cool for 2–3 minutes then brush the warmed marmalade over the top of each cupcake. Serve with crème fraîche.

queen cupcakes

MAKES 18

115 g/4 oz butter, softened

115 g/4 oz caster sugar

2 large eggs, lightly beaten

4 tsp lemon juice

175 g/6 oz self-raising flour, sifted

115 g/4 oz currants

2–4 tbsp milk, if necessary

1 Preheat the oven to 190°C/375°F/Gas Mark 5. Put 18 paper baking cases in 2 bun trays, or 18 double-layer paper cases on a baking tray.

2 Put the butter and sugar in a bowl and beat together until light and fluffy. Gradually beat in the eggs, then beat in the lemon juice with 1 tablespoon of the flour. Using a metal spoon, fold in the remaining flour and the currants, adding a little milk, if necessary, to give a soft dropping consistency. Spoon the mixture into the paper cases.

3 Bake the cupcakes in the preheated oven for 15–20 minutes, or until well risen and golden brown. Transfer to a wire rack and leave to cool.

teatime cupcakes

MAKES 10

175 g/6 oz unsalted butter, softened, plus extra for greasing

175 g/6 oz plain white flour

1 tbsp baking powder

½ tsp ground mixed spice

175 g/6 oz golden caster sugar

3 eggs, beaten

1 tsp vanilla extract

2 tbsp strong Earl Grey tea

55 g/2 oz currants

icing sugar and mixed spice, for dusting

1 Preheat the oven to 180°C/350°/Gas Mark 4. Grease ten 200-ml/7-fl oz ovenproof teacups with butter and put on 2 baking trays.

2 Sift the flour, baking powder and mixed spice into a large bowl and add the butter, caster sugar, eggs and vanilla extract. Beat well until the mixture is smooth, then stir in the tea and half the currants. Spoon the mixture into the cups and sprinkle with the remaining currants.

3 Bake the cupcakes in the preheated oven for 20–25 minutes, or until golden brown and firm to the touch. Turn out the cupcakes onto a wire rack and leave to cool.

4 Dust the cupcakes with a little icing sugar and mixed spice before serving.

sugar & spice cupcakes

MAKES 14

115 g/4 oz butter, softened

115 g/4 oz golden caster sugar

2 eggs, lightly beaten

115 g/4 oz self-raising flour

2 tsp ground mixed spice

40 g/1½ oz mixed peel

40 g/1½ oz glacé cherries, chopped

1 tbsp milk

4 white sugar cubes, roughly crushed

icing

2 tbsp granulated sugar

3 tbsp water

1 Preheat the oven to 190°C/375°F/Gas Mark 5. Put 14 paper baking cases in 2 bun trays or put 14 double-layer paper cases on a baking tray.

2 Put the butter and sugar in a bowl and beat together until light and fluffy. Gradually beat in the eggs. Sift in the flour and half the mixed spice and, using a metal spoon, fold gently into the mixture with the mixed peel, cherries and milk. Spoon the mixture into the paper cases.

3 Mix together the crushed sugar cubes and remaining mixed spice and sprinkle over the top of the cupcakes.

4 Bake the cupcakes in the preheated oven for 15–20 minutes or until risen and firm to the touch. Transfer to a wire rack.

5 To make the icing, place the sugar and water in a small pan and heat until the sugar dissolves. Bring to the boil and boil, without stirring, for 2–3 minutes until reduced and syrupy. Brush the hot syrup over the warm cupcakes. Leave to cool.

jammy cupcakes

MAKES 28

175 g/6 oz plain flour

1 tbsp baking powder

1 tbsp custard powder

175 g/6 oz unsalted butter, softened

175 g/6 oz golden caster sugar

3 eggs, beaten

1 tsp vanilla extract

70 g/2½ oz raspberry jam

icing sugar, for dusting

1 Preheat the oven to 190°C/375°F/Gas Mark 5. Place 28 paper cases into bun tins or put 28 double-layer paper cases onto baking trays.

2 Sift the flour, baking powder and custard powder into a large bowl and add the butter, caster sugar, eggs and vanilla extract. Beat well until the mixture is smooth.

3 Divide the mixture between the paper cases and place a half teaspoonful of jam onto the centre of each, without pressing down.

4 Bake in the preheated oven for 15–20 minutes, or until risen, firm and golden brown. Transfer the cupcakes to a wire rack to cool. Dust with sifted icing sugar before serving.

frosted peanut butter cupcakes

MAKES 16

55 g/2 oz butter, softened

225 g/8 oz soft light brown sugar

115 g/4 oz crunchy peanut butter

2 eggs, lightly beaten

1 tsp vanilla extract

225 g/8 oz plain flour

2 tsp baking powder

100 ml/3½ fl oz milk

chopped unsalted peanuts, to decorate

frosting

200 g/7 oz full-fat soft cream cheese

25 g/1 oz butter, softened

225 g/8 oz icing sugar

1 Preheat the oven to 180°C/350°F/Gas Mark 4. Put 16 paper baking cases in 2 bun trays or put 16 double-layer paper cases on a baking tray.

2 Put the butter, sugar and peanut butter in a bowl and beat together for 1–2 minutes, or until well mixed. Gradually add the eggs, beating well after each addition, then add the vanilla extract. Sift in the flour and baking powder and then, using a metal spoon, fold them into the mixture, alternating with the milk. Spoon the mixture into the paper cases.

3 Bake the cupcakes in the preheated oven for 25 minutes, or until well risen and golden brown. Transfer to a wire rack and leave to cool.

4 To make the frosting, put the cream cheese and butter in a bowl and beat together until smooth. Sift the icing sugar into the mixture and mix well. Put the icing in a piping bag, fitted with a large star nozzle. When the cupcakes are cold, pipe a blob on top of each cupcake and decorate with the peanuts.

chewy flapjack cupcakes

MAKES 8

40 g/1½ oz soft tub margarine

40 g/1½ oz demerara sugar

1 tbsp golden syrup

55 g/2 oz rolled oats

55 g/2 oz butter, softened

55 g/2 oz golden caster sugar

1 large egg, lightly beaten

55 g/2 oz self-raising flour

1 Preheat the oven to 190°C/375°F/Gas Mark 5. Put 8 paper baking cases in a bun tray or put 8 double-layer paper cases on a baking tray.

2 Place the margarine, demerara sugar and golden syrup in a small saucepan and heat gently until the margarine has melted. Stir in the oats. Set aside.

3 Put the butter and sugar in a bowl and beat together until light and fluffy. Gradually beat in the egg. Sift in the flour and, using a metal spoon, fold gently into the mixture. Spoon the mixture into the paper cases. Gently spoon the flapjack mixture over the top.

4 Bake the cupcakes in the preheated oven for 20 minutes or until golden brown. Transfer to a wire rack and leave to cool.

cherry bakewell cupcakes

MAKES 4

55 g/2 oz butter, softened, plus extra for greasing

55 g/2 oz caster sugar

1 large egg, lightly beaten

55 g/2 oz self-raising flour

40 g/1½ oz ground almonds

½ tsp almond extract

1 tbsp milk

40 g/1½ oz glacé cherries, quartered

1 tbsp toasted flaked almonds, to decorate

icing

40 g/1½ oz icing sugar

2 tsp lemon juice

1 Preheat the oven to 180°C/350°F/Gas Mark 4. Grease four 200-ml/7-fl oz ovenproof teacups or dishes (such as ramekins) with butter.

2 Put the butter and sugar in a bowl and beat together until light and fluffy. Gradually beat in the egg. Sift in the flour and, using a metal spoon, fold into the mixture with the ground almonds, almond extract and milk. Spoon the mixture into the teacups or dishes. Scatter over the cherries.

3 Put the cups or dishes on a baking sheet and bake in the preheated oven for 25–30 minutes or until risen, golden brown and firm to the touch. Leave to cool.

4 To make the icing, sift the icing sugar into a bowl and stir in the lemon juice to make a smooth icing. Using a teaspoon, drizzle the icing over the cupcakes and decorate with flaked almonds. Leave to set.

gingerbread cupcakes

MAKES 30

175 g/6 oz plain flour

1 tbsp baking powder

2 tsp ground ginger

1 tsp ground cinnamon

175 g/6 oz unsalted butter, softened

175 g/6 oz dark muscovado sugar

3 eggs, beaten

1 tsp vanilla extract

chopped crystallized ginger, to decorate

frosting

85 g/3 oz unsalted butter, softened

150 g/5½ oz icing sugar, sifted

3 tbsp orange juice

1 Preheat the oven to 190°C/375°F/Gas Mark 5. Place 30 paper cases into bun tins or put 30 double-layer paper cases onto baking trays.

2 Sift the flour, baking powder, ginger and cinnamon into a large bowl and add the butter, muscovado sugar, eggs and vanilla extract. Beat well until the mixture is smooth.

3 Divide the mixture between the paper cases. Bake in the preheated oven for 15–20 minutes, or until risen, firm and golden brown. Transfer the cupcakes to a wire rack to cool.

4 For the frosting, beat together the butter, icing sugar and orange juice until smooth. Spoon a little frosting on top of each cupcake and top with the crystallized ginger.

marzipan chunk cupcakes

MAKES 32

175 g/6 oz plain flour

2 tsp cornflour

1 tbsp baking powder

175 g/6 oz unsalted butter, softened

175 g/6 oz caster sugar

3 eggs, beaten

1 tsp almond extract

85 g/3 oz golden marzipan, cut into 5-mm/ ¼-inch dice

1 Preheat the oven to 190°C/375°F/Gas Mark 5. Place 32 paper cases into bun tins or put 32 double-layer paper cases onto baking trays.

2 Sift the flour, cornflour and baking powder into a large bowl and add the butter, sugar, eggs and almond extract. Beat well until the mixture is smooth.

3 Divide the mixture between the paper cases and scatter a few pieces of marzipan on top of each. Bake in the preheated oven for 15–20 minutes, or until risen, firm and golden brown. Transfer the cupcakes to a wire rack to cool.

VARIATION

To add a vanilla buttercream frosting to the cupcakes, beat together 150 g/5½ oz unsalted butter, 300 g/10½ oz icing sugar and ½ tsp vanilla extract until smooth. Spread or pipe the buttercream on the top of each cake.

2

Dreamy Chocolate

chocolate flake cupcakes

MAKES 30

175 g/6 oz plain flour

1 tbsp baking powder

175 g/6 oz unsalted butter, softened

175 g/6 oz golden caster sugar

3 eggs, beaten

1 tsp vanilla extract

2 tbsp milk

1 tbsp cocoa powder, sifted

70 g/2½ oz chocolate flake bars, crumbled

3 tbsp apricot jam, warmed

1 Preheat the oven to 190°C/375°/Gas Mark 5. Put 30 paper baking cases into bun tins or put 30 double-layer cases onto baking trays.

2 Sift the flour and baking powder into a large bowl and add the butter, sugar, eggs and vanilla extract. Beat well until the mixture is smooth. Mix the milk with the cocoa powder and stir into the mixture. Spoon the mixture into the paper cases and sprinkle with about a quarter of the crumbled chocolate.

3 Bake the cupcakes in the preheated oven for 15–20 minutes, or until golden brown and firm to the touch. Transfer the cupcakes to a wire rack and leave to cool.

4 When the cupcakes are cold, brush the tops with apricot jam and sprinkle with the remaining crumbled chocolate.

chocolate butterfly cupcakes

MAKES 12

125 g/4½ oz soft tub margarine

125 g/4½ oz caster sugar

150 g/5½ oz self-raising flour, sifted

2 large eggs

2 tbsp cocoa powder, sifted

25 g/1 oz plain chocolate, melted

icing sugar, sifted, for dusting

frosting

35 g/3 oz butter, softened

175 g/6 oz icing sugar

25 g/1 oz plain chocolate, melted

1 Preheat the oven to 180°C/350°F/Gas Mark 4. Put 12 paper baking cases in a bun tray, or put 12 double-layer paper cases on a baking tray.

2 Put the margarine, sugar, flour, eggs and cocoa powder in a large bowl and, using an electric hand whisk, beat together until just smooth. Beat in the melted chocolate. Spoon the mixture into the paper cases, filling them three-quarters full.

3 Bake the cupcakes in the preheated oven for 15 minutes, or until springy to the touch. Transfer to a wire rack and leave to cool.

4 To make the frosting, put the butter in a bowl and beat until fluffy. Sift in the icing sugar and beat together until smooth. Add the melted chocolate and beat together until well mixed.

5 When the cupcakes are cold, use a serrated knife to cut a circle from the top of each cake and then cut each circle in half. Spread or pipe a little of the frosting onto the centre of each cupcake and press 2 semi-circular halves into it at an angle to resemble butterfly wings. Dust with sifted icing sugar before serving.

molten-centred chocolate cupcakes

MAKES 8

55 g/2 oz soft tub margarine

55 g/2 oz caster sugar

1 large egg

85 g/3 oz self-raising flour, sifted

1 tbsp cocoa powder, sifted

55 g/2 oz plain chocolate

icing sugar, sifted, for dusting

1 Preheat the oven to 190°C/375°F/Gas Mark 5. Put 8 paper baking cases in a bun tray, or put 8 double-layer paper cases on a baking tray.

2 Put the margarine, sugar, egg, flour and cocoa powder in a large bowl and, using an electric hand whisk, beat together until just smooth.

3 Spoon half of the mixture into the paper cases. Using a teaspoon, make an indentation in the centre of each cake. Break the chocolate evenly into 8 squares and place a piece in each indentation, then spoon the remaining cake mixture on top.

4 Bake the cupcakes in the preheated oven for 20 minutes, or until well risen and springy to the touch. Leave the cupcakes for 2–3 minutes before serving warm, dusted with sifted icing sugar.

frosted chocolate cupcakes

MAKES 14

115 g/4 oz butter, softened

115 g/4 oz caster sugar

2 large eggs, beaten

115 g/4 oz self-raising flour, sifted

½ tsp baking powder

1½ tbsp cocoa powder, sifted

55 g/2 oz plain chocolate, melted

chocolate shapes and edible gold balls, to decorate

frosting

150 g/5½ oz plain chocolate, finely chopped

200 ml/7 fl oz double cream

140 g/5 oz unsalted butter, softened

280 g/10 oz icing sugar

1 Preheat the oven to 180°C/350°F/Gas Mark 4. Put 14 paper baking cases in a bun tray or put 14 double-layer cases on a large baking tray.

2 Place the butter, sugar, eggs, flour, baking powder and cocoa in a bowl and using an electric whisk, beat together until pale and creamy. Fold in the melted chocolate. Spoon the mixture into the paper cases. Bake the cupcakes in the preheated oven for 15–20 minutes until risen and firm to the touch. Transfer to a wire rack and leave to cool.

3 To make the frosting, put the chocolate in a heatproof bowl. Heat the cream in a saucepan until boiling then pour over the chocolate and stir until smooth. Leave to cool for 20 minutes, stirring occasionally, until thickened. Put the butter in a bowl and gradually beat in the icing sugar until smooth. Beat in the chocolate mixture. Chill for 15–20 minutes. Spoon the frosting into a piping bag fitted with a large star nozzle and pipe swirls on top of each cake. Decorate with the chocolate shapes and gold balls.

double chocolate cupcakes

MAKES 18

85 g/3 oz white chocolate
1 tbsp milk
115 g/4 oz self-raising flour
½ tsp baking powder
115 g/4 oz butter, softened
115 g/4 oz caster sugar
2 eggs
1 tsp vanilla extract

topping

140 g/5 oz milk chocolate
18 white chocolate buttons

1 Preheat the oven to 190°C/375°F/Gas Mark 5. Put 18 paper baking cases in 2 bun trays, or put 18 double-layer paper cases on a large baking tray.

2 Break the white chocolate into a heatproof bowl and add the milk. Set the bowl over a saucepan of simmering water and heat until melted. Remove from the heat and stir gently until smooth.

3 Sift the flour and baking powder into a bowl. Add the butter, sugar, eggs and vanilla extract and beat together until smooth. Fold in the melted white chocolate. Spoon the mixture into the paper cases.

4 Bake the cupcakes in the preheated oven for 20 minutes, or until golden brown and firm to the touch. Transfer the cupcakes to a wire rack and leave to cool.

5 To make the topping, break the chocolate into a heatproof bowl and set the bowl over a saucepan of gently simmering water until melted. Cool for 5 minutes then spread over the top of the cupcakes. Decorate each cupcake with a chocolate button.

chocolate brownie cupcakes

MAKES 12

225 g/8 oz plain chocolate, broken into pieces

85 g/3 oz butter

2 large eggs

200 g/7 oz soft dark brown sugar

1 tsp vanilla extract

140 g/5 oz plain flour, sifted

75g/2 ¾ oz walnuts, chopped into small pieces

1 Preheat the oven to 180°C/350°F/Gas Mark 4. Put 12 paper muffin cases in a muffin tray.

2 Place the chocolate and butter in a saucepan and heat gently, stirring constantly, until melted. Remove from the heat and stir until smooth. Leave to cool slightly.

3 Place the eggs and sugar in a large bowl and whisk together, then add the vanilla extract. Stir in the flour until mixed together, then stir the melted chocolate into the mixture until combined. Stir in the chopped walnuts. Spoon the mixture into the paper cases.

4 Bake in the preheated oven for 30 minutes, or until firm to the touch but still slightly moist in the centre. Leave the cupcakes to cool for 10 minutes, then transfer to a wire rack to cool completely.

devil's food cupcakes

MAKES 18

50 g/1 ¾ oz soft tub margarine

115 g/4 oz soft dark brown sugar

2 large eggs

115 g/4 oz plain flour, sifted

½ tsp bicarbonate of soda

25 g/1 oz cocoa powder, sifted

125 ml/4 fl oz soured cream

icing

125 g/4½ oz plain chocolate

2 tbsp caster sugar

150 ml/5 fl oz soured cream

chocolate caraque, to decorate

1 Preheat the oven to 180°C/350°F/Gas Mark 4. Put 18 paper baking cases in 2 bun trays, or put 18 double-layer paper cases on a baking tray.

2 Put the margarine, sugar, eggs, flour, bicarbonate of soda and cocoa powder in a large bowl and, using an electric hand whisk, beat together until just smooth. Using a metal spoon, fold in the soured cream. Spoon the mixture into the paper cases.

3 Bake the cupcakes in the preheated oven for 20 minutes, or until well risen and firm to the touch. Transfer to a wire rack to cool.

4 To make the icing, break the chocolate into a heatproof bowl. Set the bowl over a saucepan of gently simmering water and heat until melted, stirring occasionally. Remove from the heat and allow to cool slightly, then whisk in the sugar and soured cream until combined. Spread the icing over the tops of the cupcakes and leave to set in the refrigerator before serving. Serve decorated with chocolate caraque.

chocolate curl cupcakes

MAKES 18

85 g/3 oz butter, softened

100 g/3½ oz caster sugar

2 eggs, lightly beaten

2 tbsp milk

55 g/2 oz plain chocolate chips

225 g/8 oz self-raising flour

25 g/1 oz cocoa powder

icing

225 g/8 oz white chocolate

150 g/5½ oz low-fat cream cheese

chocolate curls, to decorate

1 Preheat the oven to 200°C/400°F/Gas Mark 6. Put 18 paper baking cases in 2 bun trays, or put 18 double-layer paper cases on a baking tray.

2 Put the butter and sugar in a bowl and beat together until light and fluffy. Gradually add the eggs, beating well after each addition. Add the milk, then fold in the chocolate chips. Sift the flour and cocoa powder together, then fold into the mixture. Spoon the mixture into the paper cases.

3 Bake the cupcakes in the preheated oven for 20 minutes, or until well risen and springy to the touch. Transfer to a wire rack and leave to cool.

4 To make the icing, break the chocolate into a heatproof bowl and set the bowl over a saucepan of simmering water until melted. Leave to cool slightly. Put the cream cheese in a bowl and beat until softened, then beat in the chocolate. Spread a little of the icing over the top of each cupcake, then leave to chill in the refrigerator for 1 hour before serving. Serve decorated with the chocolate curls.

honeycomb cupcakes

MAKES 30

175 g/6 oz plain white flour

1 tbsp baking powder

175 g/6 oz unsalted butter, softened

175 g/6 oz golden caster sugar

3 eggs, beaten

1 tsp vanilla extract

40 g/1½ oz chocolate-covered honeycomb, finely chopped

topping

200 g/7 oz icing sugar, sifted

2 tsp cocoa powder

about 2 tbsp water

40 g/1½ oz chocolate-covered honeycomb, cut into chunks

1 Preheat the oven to 190°C/375°/Gas Mark 5. Put 30 paper baking cases into bun tins or put 30 double-layer cases onto baking trays.

2 Sift the flour and baking powder into a large bowl and add the butter, caster sugar, eggs and vanilla extract. Beat well until the mixture is smooth, then stir in the chopped honeycomb. Spoon the mixture into the paper cases.

3 Bake the cupcakes in the preheated oven for 15–20 minutes, or until golden brown and firm to the touch. Transfer the cupcakes to a wire rack and leave to cool.

4 To make the topping, mix together the icing sugar, cocoa and water to make a smooth paste. Spoon a little on top of each cupcake and top with chunks of honeycomb. Leave to set.

rocky road cupcakes

MAKES 12

2 tbsp cocoa powder

2 tbsp hot water

115 g/4 oz butter, softened

115 g/4 oz caster sugar

2 eggs, lightly beaten

115 g/4 oz self-raising flour

topping

25 g/1 oz chopped mixed nuts

100 g/3½ oz milk chocolate, melted

115 g/4 oz mini marshmallows

40 g/1½ oz glacé cherries, chopped

1 Preheat the oven to 180°C/350°F/Gas Mark 4. Put 12 paper muffin cases in a muffin tray.

2 Blend the cocoa powder and hot water together and set aside. Put the butter and sugar in a bowl and beat together until light and fluffy. Gradually beat in the eggs then beat in the blended cocoa. Sift in the flour and, using a metal spoon, fold gently into the mixture. Spoon the mixture into the paper cases.

3 Bake the cupcakes in the preheated oven for 20 minutes or until risen and firm to the touch. Transfer to a wire rack and leave to cool.

4 To make the topping, stir the nuts into the melted chocolate and spread a little of the mixture over the top of the cakes. Lightly stir the marshmallows and cherries into the remaining chocolate mixture and pile on top of the cupcakes. Leave to set.

dark & white fudge cupcakes

MAKES 20

200 ml/7 fl oz water
85 g/3 oz butter, softened
85 g/3 oz caster sugar
1 tbsp golden syrup
3 tbsp milk
1 tsp vanilla extract
1 tsp bicarbonate of soda
225 g/8 oz plain flour
2 tbsp cocoa powder

icing

50 g/1 ¾ oz plain chocolate
4 tbsp water
50 g/1¾ oz butter
50 g/1¾ oz white chocolate
350 g/12 oz icing sugar

chocolate curls

100 g/3½ oz plain chocolate
100 g/3½ oz white chocolate

1 Preheat the oven to 180°C/350°F/Gas Mark 4. Put 20 paper baking cases in 2 bun trays, or put 20 double-layer paper cases on 2 baking trays.

2 Put the water, butter, sugar and syrup in a saucepan. Heat gently, stirring, until the sugar has dissolved, then bring to the boil. Reduce the heat and cook gently for 5 minutes. Remove from the heat and leave to cool.

3 Meanwhile, put the milk and vanilla extract in a bowl. Add the bicarbonate of soda and stir to dissolve. Sift the flour and cocoa powder into a separate bowl and add the syrup mixture. Stir in the milk and beat until smooth. Spoon the mixture into the paper cases until they are two-thirds full.

4 Bake the cupcakes in the preheated oven for 20 minutes, or until well risen and firm to the touch. Transfer to a wire rack and leave to cool.

5 To make the topping, break the plain chocolate into a small heatproof bowl, add half the water and half the butter, and set the bowl over a saucepan of gently simmering water until melted. Stir until smooth and leave to stand over the water. Repeat with the white chocolate and remaining water and butter. Sift half the icing sugar into each bowl and beat until smooth and thick. Top up the cupcakes with the icings. Leave to set. Serve decorated with chocolate curls made by shaving the chocolate with a potato peeler.

white chocolate & rose cupcakes

MAKES 12

115 g/4 oz unsalted butter

115 g/4 oz caster sugar

1 tsp rose water

2 eggs, beaten

115 g/4 oz self-raising flour

55 g/2 oz white chocolate, grated

sugar frosted pink rose petals, to decorate

frosting

115 g/4 oz white chocolate, broken into pieces

2 tbsp milk

175 g/6 oz full-fat soft cheese

25 g/1 oz icing sugar, sifted

1 Preheat the oven to 180°C/350°F/Gas Mark 4. Put 12 paper baking cases in a bun tray or put 12 double-layer cases on a large baking tray.

2 Place the butter, sugar and rose water in a bowl and beat together until pale and creamy. Gradually beat in the eggs. Sift over the flour and fold in gently. Fold in the white chocolate. Spoon the mixture into the paper cases.

3 Bake the cupcakes in the preheated oven for 15–20 minutes, or until golden brown and firm to the touch. Transfer the cupcakes to a wire rack and leave to cool.

4 To make the frosting, place the chocolate and milk in a heatproof bowl set over a pan of simmering water and leave until melted. Remove from the heat and stir until smooth. Cool for 30 minutes. Put the soft cheese and icing sugar in a bowl and beat together until smooth and creamy. Fold in the chocolate. Chill in the refrigerator for 1 hour. Swirl the frosting over the top of the cupcakes. Decorate with the sugar frosted rose petals.

peppermint cupcakes

MAKES 32

175 g/6 oz plain white flour

1 tbsp baking powder

175 g/6 oz unsalted butter, softened

175 g/6 oz caster sugar

3 eggs, beaten

1 tsp peppermint extract

70 g/2½ oz plain chocolate chips

topping

100 g/3½ oz plain chocolate, melted

10 chocolate mint sticks, broken into short lengths

1 Preheat the oven to 190°C/375°/Gas Mark 5. Put 32 paper baking cases into bun tins or put 32 double-layer cases onto baking trays.

2 Sift the flour and baking powder into a large bowl and add the butter, sugar, eggs and peppermint extract. Beat well until the mixture is smooth, then stir in half the chocolate chips. Spoon the mixture into the paper cases and sprinkle with the remaining chocolate chips.

3 Bake the cupcakes in the preheated oven for 15–20 minutes, or until golden brown and firm to the touch. Transfer the cupcakes to a wire rack and leave to cool.

4 When cooled, drizzle the cupcakes with the melted chocolate and decorate with pieces of chocolate mint stick. Leave to set.

chocolate & nut cupcakes

MAKES 18

175 g/6 oz butter, softened

115 g/4 oz light soft brown sugar

2 large eggs, lightly beaten

2 tbsp chocolate and hazelnut spread

175 g/6 oz self-raising flour

50 g/2 oz blanched hazelnuts, roughly ground

topping

5 tbsp chocolate and hazelnut spread

18 whole blanched hazelnuts

1 Preheat the oven to 180°C/350°F/Gas Mark 4. Put 18 paper baking cases in 2 bun trays or put 18 double-layer paper cases on a large baking tray.

2 Put the butter and sugar in a mixing bowl and beat together until light and fluffy. Gradually beat in the eggs then stir in the chocolate and hazelnut spread. Sift in the flour and, using a metal spoon, fold into the mixture with the ground hazelnuts. Spoon the mixture into the paper cases.

3 Bake the cupcakes in the preheated oven for 20–25 minutes or until risen and firm to the touch. Transfer to a wire rack and leave to cool.

4 When the cupcakes are cold, swirl some chocolate and hazelnut spread over the top of each cupcake and top with a hazelnut.

hot pecan brownie cupcakes

MAKES 6

115 g/4 oz butter, plus extra for greasing

115 g/4 oz plain chocolate, broken into pieces

2 eggs

115 g/4 oz soft light brown sugar

3 tbsp maple syrup

115 g/4 oz plain flour, sifted

55 g/2 oz pecan nuts, chopped

crème fraiche, to serve

1 Preheat the oven to 180°C/350°F/Gas Mark 4. Grease six 150-ml/5-fl oz ovenproof teacups or dishes (such as ramekins) with butter.

2 Put the chocolate and butter into a heatproof bowl set over a saucepan of gently simmering water and leave until melted, stirring occasionally. Cool for 5 minutes.

3 Put the eggs, sugar and maple syrup in a bowl and whisk together until well blended. Whisk in the chocolate mixture, and then fold in the flour and two thirds of the pecan nuts. Pour the mixture into the cups or dishes and scatter over the rest of the nuts.

4 Put the cups or dishes on a baking sheet and bake in the preheated oven for 25–30 minutes or until the cupcakes are risen and crisp on top but still feel slightly wobbly if lightly pressed. Serve hot, topped with a spoonful of crème fraiche.

mocha cupcakes

MAKES 20

2 tbsp instant espresso coffee powder

85 g/3 oz butter, softened

85 g/3 oz caster sugar

1 tbsp clear honey

200 ml/7 fl oz water

225 g/8 oz plain flour

2 tbsp cocoa powder

1 tsp bicarbonate of soda

3 tbsp milk

1 large egg, lightly beaten

topping

225 ml/8 fl oz whipping cream

cocoa powder, sifted, for dusting

1 Preheat the oven to 180°C/350°F/Gas Mark 4. Put 20 paper baking cases in 2 bun trays, or put 20 double-layer paper cases on 2 baking trays.

2 Put the coffee powder, butter, sugar, honey and water in a saucepan and heat gently, stirring, until the sugar has dissolved. Bring to the boil, then reduce the heat and simmer for 5 minutes. Pour into a large heatproof bowl and leave to cool.

3 When the mixture has cooled, sift in the flour and cocoa powder. Dissolve the bicarbonate of soda in the milk, then add to the mixture with the egg and beat together until smooth. Spoon the mixture into the paper cases. Bake the cupcakes in the preheated oven for 15–20 minutes, or until well risen and firm to the touch. Transfer to a wire rack to cool.

4 To make the topping, whisk the cream in a bowl until it hold its shape. Spoon a teaspoonful of cream on top of each cupcake, then dust with cocoa powder.

chocolate & orange cupcakes

MAKES 16

115 g/4 oz butter, softened

115 g/4 oz golden caster sugar

finely grated rind and juice ½ orange

2 eggs, lightly beaten

115 g/4 oz self-raising flour

25 g/1 oz plain chocolate, grated

icing

115 g/4 oz plain chocolate, broken into pieces

25 g/1 oz unsalted butter

1 tbsp golden syrup

thin strips candied orange peel, to decorate

1 Preheat the oven to 180°C/350°F/Gas Mark 4. Put 16 paper baking cases in 2 bun trays or put 16 double-layer paper cases on a baking tray.

2 Put the butter, sugar and orange rind in a bowl and beat together until light and fluffy. Gradually beat in the eggs. Sift in the flour and, using a metal spoon, fold gently into the mixture with the orange juice and grated chocolate. Spoon the mixture into the paper cases.

3 Bake the cupcakes in the preheated oven for 20 minutes or until risen and golden brown. Transfer to a wire rack and leave to cool.

4 To make the icing, break the chocolate into a heatproof bowl and add the butter and syrup. Set the bowl over a saucepan of simmering water and heat until melted. Remove from the heat and stir until smooth. Cool until the icing is thick enough to spread. Spread over the cupcakes and decorate each cupcake with a few strips of candied orange peel. Leave to set.

black forest cupcakes

MAKES 12

85 g/3 oz plain chocolate

1 tsp lemon juice

4 tbsp milk

150 g/5½ oz self-raising flour

1 tbsp cocoa powder

½ tsp bicarbonate of soda

2 eggs

55 g/2 oz butter, softened

115 g/4 oz soft light brown sugar

25 g/1 oz dried and sweetened sour cherries, chopped

2 tbsp cherry liqueur (optional)

150 ml/5 fl oz double cream, softly whipped

5 tbsp cherry jam

cocoa powder, to dust

1 Preheat the oven to 180°C/350°F/Gas Mark 4. Put 12 paper muffin cases in a muffin tray.

2 Break the chocolate into a heatproof bowl and set the bowl over a saucepan of gently simmering water until melted. Add the lemon juice to the milk and leave for 10 minutes – the milk will curdle a little.

3 Sift the flour, cocoa powder and bicarbonate of soda into a bowl. Add the eggs, butter, sugar and milk mixture and beat with an electric hand whisk until smooth. Fold in the melted chocolate and cherries. Spoon the mixture into the paper cases.

4 Bake the cupcakes in the preheated oven for 20–25 minutes until risen and firm to the touch. Transfer to a wire rack and leave to cool.

5 When the cupcakes are cold, use a serrated knife to cut a circle from the top of each cupcake. Sprinkle the cakes with a little cherry liqueur, if using. Spoon the whipped cream onto the centres and top with a small spoonful of jam. Gently replace the cupcake tops and dust lightly with cocoa powder. Store in the refrigerator until ready to serve.

pear & chocolate cupcakes

MAKES 12

115 g/4 oz soft tub margarine

115 g/4 oz light soft brown sugar

2 eggs

100 g/3½ oz self-raising flour, sifted

½ tsp baking powder

2 tbsp cocoa powder, sifted

4 canned pear halves, drained and sliced

2 tbsp runny honey, warmed

1 Preheat the oven to 190°C/375°F/Gas Mark 5. Put 12 paper baking cases in a bun tray or put 12 double-layer paper cases on a baking tray.

2 Put the margarine, sugar, eggs, flour, baking powder and cocoa powder in a large bowl and, using an electric hand whisk, beat together until just smooth. Spoon the mixture into the paper cases and smooth the tops. Arrange 2 pear slices on top of each cupcake.

3 Bake the cupcakes in the preheated oven for 20 minutes or until risen and just firm to the touch. Transfer to a wire cooling rack. Whilst the cupcakes are still warm, glaze with the honey. Leave to cool completely.

chocolate chip cupcakes

MAKES 8

100 g/3½ oz soft tub margarine

100 g/3½ oz caster sugar

2 large eggs

100 g/3½ oz self-raising flour, sifted

100 g/3½ oz plain chocolate chips

1 Preheat the oven to 190°C/375°F/Gas Mark 5. Put 8 paper baking cases in a bun tray or put 8 double-layer paper cases on a baking tray.

2 Put the margarine, sugar, eggs and flour in a large bowl and, using an electric hand whisk, beat together until just smooth. Fold in the chocolate chips. Spoon the mixture into the paper cases.

3 Bake the cupcakes in the preheated oven for 20–25 minutes, or until well risen and golden brown. Transfer to a wire rack to cool.

white chocolate chip cupcakes

175 g/6 oz plain white flour

1 tbsp baking powder

175 g/6 oz unsalted butter, softened

175 g/6 oz golden caster sugar

3 eggs, beaten

1 tsp vanilla extract

70 g/2½ oz white chocolate chips

topping

100 g/3½ oz white chocolate, melted

2 tbsp dark chocolate sprinkles

1 Preheat the oven to 190°C/375°/Gas Mark 5. Put 32 paper baking cases into bun tins or put 32 double-layer cases onto baking trays.

2 Sift the flour and baking powder into a large bowl and add the butter, sugar, eggs and vanilla extract. Beat well until the mixture is smooth, then stir in half the chocolate chips. Spoon the mixture into the paper cases and sprinkle with the remaining chocolate chips

3 Bake the cupcakes in the preheated oven for 15–20 minutes, or until golden brown and firm to the touch. Transfer the cupcakes to a wire rack and leave to cool.

4 When the cupcakes are cold, spoon a little melted white chocolate on top of each and scatter over the chocolate sprinkles. Leave to set.

chocolate fruit & nut cupcakes

MAKES 12

55 g/2 oz plain chocolate

85 g/3 oz butter, softened

1 tbsp golden syrup

55 g/2 oz light soft brown sugar

115 g/4 oz self-raising flour

1 large egg, beaten

topping

40 g/1½ oz glace cherries, chopped

25 g/1 oz flaked almonds

1 tbsp raisins

1 tbsp golden syrup

1 Preheat the oven to 190°C/375°F/Gas Mark 5. Put 12 paper baking cases in a bun tray or put 12 double-layer paper cases on a baking tray.

2 Put the chocolate, butter, golden syrup and sugar in a saucepan and heat gently, stirring occasionally, until just melted. Cool for 2 minutes. Sift the flour into a bowl.

3 Pour the chocolate mixture into the bowl. Add the egg and beat until thoroughly blended. Spoon the mixture into the paper cases.

4 Mix together the topping ingredients and gently spoon a little of the mixture on top of each cupcake.

5 Bake the cupcakes in the preheated oven for 15–20 minutes or until risen and firm to the touch. Transfer to a wire rack and leave to cool.

tiny chocolate cupcakes

MAKES 20

55 g/2 oz butter, softened

55 g/2 oz caster sugar

1 large egg, lightly beaten

55 g/2 oz self-raising flour

2 tbsp cocoa powder

1 tbsp milk

20 chocolate-coated coffee beans, to decorate (optional)

icing

100 g/3½ oz plain chocolate

100 ml/3½ fl oz double cream

1 Preheat the oven to 190°C/375°F/Gas Mark 5. Put 20 double-layer mini paper cases on 2 baking trays.

2 Put the butter and sugar in a bowl and beat together until light and fluffy. Gradually beat in the egg. Sift in the flour and cocoa powder and then, using a metal spoon, fold them into the mixture. Stir in the milk.

3 Fill a piping bag, fitted with a large plain nozzle, with the mixture and pipe it into the paper cases, filling each one until half full.

4 Bake the cakes in the preheated oven for 10–15 minutes, or until well risen and firm to the touch. Transfer to a wire rack to cool.

5 To make the icing, break the chocolate into a saucepan and add the cream. Heat gently, stirring all the time, until the chocolate has melted. Pour into a large heatproof bowl and, using an electric hand whisk, beat the mixture for 10 minutes, or until thick, glossy and cool.

6 Fill a piping bag, fitted with a large star nozzle, with the icing and pipe a swirl on top of each cupcake. Chill in the refrigerator for 1 hour before serving. Serve decorated with a chocolate-coated coffee bean, if desired.

marbled chocolate cupcakes

MAKES 21

175 g/6 oz soft tub margarine

175 g/6 oz caster sugar

3 eggs

175 g/6 oz self-raising flour, sifted

2 tbsp milk

55 g/2 oz plain chocolate, melted

1 Preheat the oven to 180°C/350°F/Gas Mark 4. Put 21 paper baking cases in 2 bun trays, or put 21 double-layer paper cases on 2 baking trays.

2 Put the margarine, sugar, eggs, flour and milk in a large bowl and, using an electric hand whisk, beat together until just smooth.

3 Divide the mixture between 2 bowls. Add the melted chocolate to one bowl and stir until well mixed. Using a teaspoon, and alternating the chocolate mixture with the plain mixture, put four half-teaspoons into each paper case.

4 Bake the cupcakes in the preheated oven for 20 minutes, or until well risen and springy to the touch. Transfer to a wire rack and leave to cool.

VARIATION

Add the grated rind and juice of ½ a small orange and a few drops of orange food colouring to the plain cake mixture to make chocolate orange marbled cupcakes.

3

Fabulous Fruit & Nut

lemon & raspberry cupcakes

MAKES 12

115 g/4 oz butter, softened

115 g/4 oz caster sugar

2 eggs, lightly beaten

115 g/4 oz self-raising flour

finely grated rind of 1 lemon

1 tbsp lemon curd

100 g/3½ oz fresh raspberries

topping

25 g/1 oz butter

1 tbsp soft light brown sugar

1 tbsp ground almonds

1 tbsp plain flour

1 Preheat the oven to 200°C/400°F/Gas Mark 6. Put 12 paper baking cases into bun tins or put 12 double-layer cases onto baking trays.

2 To make the topping, place the butter in a saucepan and heat gently until melted. Pour into a bowl and add the sugar, ground almonds and flour and stir together until combined.

3 To make the cupcakes, place the butter and sugar in a large bowl and beat together until light and fluffy, then gradually add the eggs. Sift in the flour and fold into the mixture. Fold in the lemon rind, lemon curd and raspberries. Spoon the mixture into the paper cases. Add the topping to cover the top of each cupcake and press down gently.

4 Bake in the preheated oven for 15–20 minutes, or until golden brown and firm to the touch. Leave the cupcakes to cool for 10 minutes, then transfer to a wire rack to cool completely.

lemon butterfly cupcakes

MAKES 12

115 g/4 oz self-raising flour

½ tsp baking powder

115 g/4 oz soft tub margarine

115 g/4 oz caster sugar

2 eggs, lightly beaten

finely grated rind of ½ lemon

2 tbsp milk

icing sugar, for dusting

frosting

85 g/3 oz butter, softened

175/6 oz icing sugar

1 tbsp lemon juice

1 Preheat the oven to 190°C/375°F/Gas Mark 5. Put 12 paper baking cases in a bun tray, or put 12 double-layer paper cases on a baking tray.

2 Sift the flour and baking powder into a large bowl. Add the margarine, sugar, eggs, lemon rind and milk and, using an electric hand whisk, beat together until smooth. Spoon the mixture into the paper cases.

3 Bake the cupcakes in the preheated oven for 15–20 minutes, or until well risen and golden brown. Transfer to a wire rack and leave to cool.

4 To make the frosting, put the butter in a bowl and beat until fluffy. Sift in the icing sugar, add the lemon juice and beat together until smooth and creamy.

5 When the cupcakes are cold, use a serrated knife to cut a circle from the top of each cupcake and then cut each circle in half. Spread or pipe a little of the frosting onto the centre of each cupcake, then press 2 semicircular halves into it at an angle to resemble butterfly wings. Dust with sifted icing sugar before serving.

lemon crunch cupcakes

MAKES 12

175 g/6 oz butter, softened

175 g/6 oz golden caster sugar

175 g/6 oz self-raising flour, sifted

1 tsp baking powder

3 large eggs

3 tbsp lemon curd

topping

100 g/3½ oz granulated sugar

juice and grated rind 1 lemon

1 Preheat the oven to 180°C/350°F/Gas Mark 4. Put 12 paper cases in a tray.

2 Put the butter, sugar, flour and baking powder and eggs in a large bowl and, using an electric hand whisk, beat until the mixture is thoroughly blended. Fold in the lemon curd. Spoon the mixture into the paper cases.

3 Bake the cupcakes in the preheated oven for 20 minutes or until risen and golden brown. While the cupcakes are baking, mix the topping ingredients together in a bowl.

4 Remove the cupcakes from the oven and leave for 2 minutes, then spread some of the topping over each cupcake. Leave to cool in the tray – the topping will go crisp on cooling.

pineapple tropical cupcakes

MAKES 12

2 slices of canned pineapple in natural juice

85 g/3 oz butter, softened

85 g/3 oz caster sugar

1 large egg, lightly beaten

85 g/3 oz self-raising flour, sifted

1 tbsp juice from the canned pineapple

frosting

25 g/1 oz butter, softened

100 g/3½ oz soft cream cheese

grated rind of 1 lemon or lime

100 g/3½ oz icing sugar

1 tsp lemon juice or lime juice

1 Preheat the oven to 180°C/350°F/Gas Mark 4. Put 12 paper baking cases in a bun tray, or put 12 double-layer paper cases on a baking tray.

2 Finely chop the pineapple slices. Put the butter and sugar in a bowl and beat together until light and fluffy. Gradually beat in the egg. Add the flour and, using a large metal spoon, fold into the mixture. Fold in the chopped pineapple and the pineapple juice. Spoon the mixture into the paper cases.

3 Bake the cupcakes in the preheated oven for 20 minutes, or until well risen and golden brown. Transfer to a wire rack and leave to cool.

4 To make the frosting, put the butter and cream cheese in a bowl and beat together until smooth. Add the lemon rind. Sift the icing sugar into the mixture, then beat together until well mixed. Gradually beat in the juice from the lemon or lime, adding enough to form a spreading consistency. Put the frosting in a piping bag fitted with a large star nozzle. When the cupcakes are cold, pipe a blob on top of each cupcake.

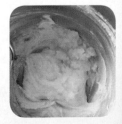

mango & passion fruit cupcakes

MAKES 18

115 g/4 oz butter, softened

115 g/4 oz caster sugar

1 tsp finely grated orange rind

2 eggs, lightly beaten

115 g/4 oz self-raising flour

55 g/2 oz dried mango, finely chopped

1 tbsp orange juice

icing

200 g/7 oz icing sugar

seeds and pulp from 1 passion fruit

2 tbsp orange juice

1 Preheat the oven to 190°C/375°F/Gas Mark 5. Put 18 paper cases into bun trays or put 18 double-layer paper cases on a baking tray.

2 Put the butter, sugar and orange rind in a mixing bowl and beat together until light and fluffy. Gradually beat in the eggs. Sift in the flour and, using a metal spoon, fold into the mixture with the chopped mango and orange juice. Spoon the mixture into the paper cases.

3 Bake the cupcakes in the preheated oven for 20 minutes or until golden brown and firm to the touch. Transfer to a wire rack and leave to cool.

4 To make the icing, sift the icing sugar into a bowl and add the passion fruit seeds and pulp and 1 tbsp of the orange juice. Mix to a smooth icing, adding the rest of the juice if necessary. Spoon the icing over the cupcakes. Leave to set.

frosted blueberry cupcakes

MAKES 30

175 g/6 oz plain flour

1 tbsp baking powder

175 g/6 oz unsalted butter, softened

175 g/6 oz caster sugar

3 eggs, beaten

1 tsp vanilla extract

finely grated rind of ½ orange

150 g/5½ oz fresh blueberries

icing

3 tbsp soured cream

150 g/5½ oz icing sugar, sifted

1 Preheat the oven to 190°C/375°/Gas Mark 5. Put 30 paper baking cases into bun tins or put 30 double-layer cases onto baking trays.

2 Sift the flour and baking powder into a large bowl and add the butter, caster sugar, eggs and vanilla extract. Beat well until the mixture is smooth, then stir in the orange rind and 100g/3½ oz of the blueberries. Spoon the mixture into the paper cases.

3 Bake the cupcakes in the preheated oven for 15–20 minutes, or until golden brown and firm to the touch. Transfer the cupcakes to a wire rack and leave to cool.

4 To make the icing, stir the soured cream into the icing sugar and mix well until smooth. Spoon a little icing on top of each cupcake and top with the remaining blueberries. Leave to set.

buttermilk cupcakes

MAKES 6

140 g/5 oz butter, softened, plus extra for greasing

140 g/5 oz caster sugar

2 eggs, lightly beaten

4 tbsp cultured buttermilk

175 g/6 oz self-raising flour

115 g/4 oz blueberries

icing sugar, for dusting

1 Preheat the oven to 190°C/375°F/Gas Mark 5. Grease six 200-ml/7-fl oz ovenproof teacups or dishes (such as ramekins) with butter.

2 Put the butter and sugar in a bowl and beat together until light and fluffy. Gradually beat in the eggs. Stir in the buttermilk. Sift in the flour and, using a metal spoon, fold into the mixture. Gently fold in half the blueberries. Spoon the mixture into the cups or dishes. Scatter over the rest of the blueberries.

3 Put the cups or dishes on a baking sheet and bake in the preheated oven for 25 minutes until risen and firm to the touch. Serve warm or cold, dusted with sifted icing sugar.

shredded orange cupcakes

MAKES 12

85 g/3 oz butter, softened

85 g/3 oz caster sugar

1 large egg, lightly beaten

85 g/3 oz self-raising flour, sifted

25 g/1 oz ground almonds

grated rind and juice of 1 small orange

orange topping

grated rind and juice of 1 small orange

55 g/2 oz caster sugar

15 g/½ oz toasted flaked almonds

1 Preheat the oven to 180°C/350°F/Gas Mark 4. Put 12 paper baking cases in a bun tray, or put 12 double-layer paper cases on a baking tray.

2 Put the butter and sugar in a bowl and beat together until light and fluffy. Gradually beat in the egg. Add the flour, ground almonds and orange rind and, using a large metal spoon, fold into the mixture. Fold in the orange juice. Spoon the mixture into the paper cases.

3 Bake the cupcakes in the preheated oven for 20–25 minutes, or until well risen and golden brown.

4 Meanwhile, make the topping. Put the orange rind, orange juice and sugar in a saucepan and heat gently, stirring, until the sugar has dissolved, then simmer for 5 minutes.

5 When the cupcakes have cooked, prick them all over with a skewer. Spoon the warm syrup and rind over each cupcake, then scatter the flaked almonds on top. Transfer to a wire rack and leave to cool.

carrot & orange cupcakes

MAKES 12

115 g/4 oz butter, softened

115 g/4 oz soft light brown sugar

juice and finely grated rind of 1 small orange

2 large eggs, lightly beaten

175 g/6 oz carrots, grated

25 g/1 oz walnut pieces, roughly chopped

125 g/4½ oz plain flour

1 tsp ground mixed spice

1½ tsp baking powder

frosting

280 g/10 oz mascarpone cheese

4 tbsp icing sugar

grated rind of 1 large orange

1 Preheat the oven to 180°C/350°F/Gas Mark 4. Put 12 paper baking cases in a bun tray or put 12 double-layer paper cases on a baking tray.

2 Put the butter, sugar and orange rind in a bowl and beat together until light and fluffy. Gradually add the eggs, beating well after each addition. Squeeze any excess liquid from the carrots and add to the mixture with the walnuts and orange juice. Stir into the mixture until well mixed. Sift the flour, mixed spice and baking powder and then, using a metal spoon, fold into the mixture. Spoon the mixture into the paper cases.

3 Bake the cupcakes in the preheated oven for 25 minutes, or until well risen, firm to the touch and golden brown. Transfer to a wire rack and leave to cool.

4 To make the frosting, put the mascarpone cheese, icing sugar and orange rind in a large bowl and beat together until well mixed.

5 When the cupcakes are cold, spread the frosting on top of each cupcake, swirling it with a round-bladed knife. Store the cupcakes in the refrigerator until ready to serve.

raspberry almond cupcakes

MAKES 14

115 g/4 oz butter, softened

85 g/3 oz caster sugar

½ tsp almond extract

2 eggs, lightly beaten

85 g/3 oz self-raising flour

55 g/2 oz ground almonds

85 g/3 oz fresh raspberries

2 tbsp flaked almonds

icing sugar, for dusting

1 Preheat the oven to 180°C/350°F/Gas Mark 4. Put 14 paper baking cases in 2 bun trays or put 14 double-layer paper cases on a baking tray.

2 Put the butter, sugar and almond extract in a bowl and beat together until light and fluffy. Gradually beat in the eggs. Sift in the flour and, using a metal spoon, fold into the mixture with the ground almonds. Gently fold in the raspberries. Spoon the mixture into the paper cases. Scatter the flaked almonds over the top.

3 Bake the cupcakes in the preheated oven for 25–30 minutes or until golden brown and firm to the touch. Transfer to a wire rack and leave to cool. Dust with icing sifted sugar.

blackberry crumble cupcakes

MAKES 6

115 g/4 oz butter, softened, plus extra for greasing

115 g/4 oz self-raising flour

½ tsp baking powder

115 g/4 oz caster sugar

2 eggs

175 g/6 oz blackberries

whipped cream or custard, to serve

crumble topping

85 g/3 oz self-raising flour

55 g/2 oz demerara sugar

55 g/2 oz butter, chilled and diced

1 Preheat the oven to 190°C/375°F/Gas Mark 5. Grease six 200-ml/7-fl oz ovenproof teacups or dishes (such as ramekins) with butter.

2 To make the topping, mix the flour and sugar in a bowl. Add the butter and rub in until the mixture resembles course breadcrumbs.

3 To make the sponge, sift the flour and baking powder into a bowl. Add the butter, caster sugar and eggs and, using an electric hand whisk, beat together until smooth. Spoon the mixture into the cups or dishes and level the surface. Top with the blackberries. Spoon the crumble topping over the blackberries.

4 Put the cups or dishes on a baking sheet and bake in the preheated oven for 25–30 minutes until the crumble topping is golden brown. Serve warm with whipped cream or custard.

hummingbird cupcakes

MAKES 12

150 g/5½ plain flour

¾ tsp bicarbonate of soda

1 tsp ground cinnamon

125 g/4½ oz soft light brown sugar

2 eggs, beaten

100 ml/3½ fl oz sunflower oil

1 ripe banana (about 85 g/3 oz peeled weight), mashed

2 canned pineapple rings, drained and finely chopped

25 g/1 oz pecan nuts, finely chopped, plus extra sliced pecan nuts to decorate

frosting

140 g/5 oz full-fat soft cheese

75 g/2½ oz unsalted butter, softened

1 tsp vanilla extract

280 g/10 oz icing sugar, sifted

1 Preheat the oven to 180°C/350°F/Gas Mark 4. Put 12 paper baking cases in a bun tray or put 12 double-layer cases on a large baking tray.

2 Sift the flour, bicarbonate of soda and cinnamon into a bowl and stir in the sugar. Add the eggs, oil, banana, pineapple and chopped pecan nuts and mix thoroughly. Spoon the mixture into the paper cases.

3 Bake the cupcakes in the preheated oven for 15–20 minutes until risen, golden and firm to the touch. Transfer to a wire rack and leave to cool.

4 To make the frosting, put the soft cheese, butter and vanilla extract in a bowl and blend together with a spatula. Beat in the icing sugar until smooth and creamy. Pipe or swirl the frosting on the top of the cupcakes. Decorate with sliced pecan nuts.

cranberry cupcakes

MAKES 14

75 g/2¾ oz butter, softened

100 g/3½ oz caster sugar

1 large egg

2 tbsp milk

100 g/3½ oz self-raising flour

1 tsp baking powder

75 g/2 ¾ oz cranberries, frozen

1 Preheat the oven to 180°C/350°F/Gas Mark 4. Put 14 paper baking cases in 2 bun trays, or put 14 double-layer paper cases on a baking tray.

2 Put the butter and sugar in a bowl and beat together until light and fluffy. Gradually beat in the egg, then stir in the milk. Sift in the flour and baking powder and, using a large metal spoon, fold them into the mixture. Gently fold in the frozen cranberries. Spoon the mixture into the paper cases.

3 Bake the cupcakes in the preheated oven for 15–20 minutes, or until well risen and golden brown. Transfer to a wire rack and leave to cool.

wholemeal apricot cupcakes

MAKES 14

115 g/4 oz butter, softened

85 g/3 oz light soft brown sugar

2 tbsp set honey

2 eggs, lightly beaten

115 g/4 oz plain wholemeal flour

1½ tsp baking powder

1 tsp ground mixed spice

85 g/3 oz ready-to-eat dried apricots, chopped

2 tbsp apricot jam, warmed and sieved

slices of ready-to-eat dried apricots, to decorate

1 Preheat the oven to 190°C/375°F/Gas Mark 5. Put 14 paper baking cases in 2 bun trays or put 14 double-layer paper cases on a baking tray.

2 Put the butter, sugar and honey in a bowl and beat together until light and fluffy. Gradually add the eggs, beating well after each addition. Sift in the flour, baking powder and mixed spice (tipping any bran left in the sieve into the bowl) and, using a metal spoon, fold them into the mixture with the chopped apricots. Spoon the mixture into the paper cases.

3 Bake the cupcakes in the preheated oven for 15–20 minutes or until risen, golden brown and firm to the touch. Transfer to a wire rack to cool.

4 When the cupcakes are cold, brush the apricot jam over the top of the cupcake and decorate each with a slice of apricot.

spiced plum cupcakes

MAKES 4

55 g/2 oz butter, softened, plus extra for greasing

55 g/2 oz caster sugar

1 large egg, lightly beaten

55 g/2 oz plain wholemeal flour

½ tsp baking powder

1 tsp ground mixed spice

25 g/1 oz blanched hazelnuts, coarsely ground

2 small plums, halved, stoned and sliced

Greek-style yogurt, to serve

1 Preheat the oven to 180°C/350°F/Gas Mark 4. Grease four 150-ml/5-fl oz ovenproof teacups or dishes (such as ramekins) with butter.

2 Put the butter and sugar in a bowl and beat together until light and fluffy. Gradually beat in the egg. Sift in the flour, baking powder and mixed spice (tipping any bran left in the sieve into the bowl) and, using a metal spoon, fold into the mixture with the ground hazelnuts. Spoon the mixture into the teacups. Arrange the sliced plums on top of the mixture.

3 Put the cups on a baking sheet and bake in the preheated oven for 25 minutes or until risen and firm to the touch. Serve warm or cold with Greek-style yogurt.

apple streusel cupcakes

MAKES 14

½ tsp bicarbonate of soda

280 g/10 oz jar Bramley apple sauce

55 g/2 oz butter, softened

85 g/3 oz demerara sugar

1 large egg, lightly beaten

175 g/6 oz self-raising flour

½ tsp ground cinnamon

½ tsp freshly ground nutmeg

topping

50 g/1 ¾ oz plain white flour

50 g/1¾ oz demerara sugar

¼ tsp ground cinnamon

¼ tsp freshly grated nutmeg

35 g/1¼ oz butter

1 Preheat the oven to 180°C/350°F/Gas Mark 4. Put 14 paper baking cases in 2 bun trays, or put 14 double-layer paper cases on a baking tray.

2 To make the topping, put the flour, sugar, cinnamon and nutmeg in a bowl. Cut the butter into small pieces, then rub in by hand until the mixture resembles fine breadcrumbs.

3 Add the bicarbonate of soda to the jar of Bramley apple sauce and stir until dissolved. Put the butter and sugar in a bowl and beat together until light and fluffy. Gradually beat in the egg. Sift in the flour, cinnamon and nutmeg and, using a large metal spoon, fold into the mixture, alternating with the apple sauce. Spoon the mixture into the paper cases. Scatter the topping over the cupcakes to cover the tops and press down gently.

4 Bake the cupcakes in the preheated oven for 20 minutes, or until well risen and golden brown. Leave the cakes for 2–3 minutes before serving warm or transfer to a wire rack and leave to cool.

coconut cherry cupcakes

MAKES 12

115 g/4 oz butter, softened

115 g/4 oz caster sugar

2 tbsp milk

2 eggs, lightly beaten

85 g/3 oz self-raising flour

½ tsp baking powder

85 g/3 oz desiccated coconut

115 g/4 oz glacé cherries, quartered

12 whole glacé, maraschino or fresh cherries, to decorate

frosting

55 g/2 oz butter, softened

115 g/4 oz icing sugar

1 tbsp milk

1 Preheat the oven to 180°C/350°F/Gas Mark 4. Put 12 paper baking cases in a bun tray, or put 12 double-layer paper cases on a baking tray.

2 Put the butter and sugar in a bowl and beat together until light and fluffy. Stir in the milk. Gradually add the eggs, beating well after each addition. Sift in the flour and baking powder and fold them in with the coconut. Gently fold in most of the quartered cherries. Spoon the mixture into the paper cases and scatter the remaining quartered cherries on top.

3 Bake the cupcakes in the preheated oven for 20–25 minutes, or until well risen, golden brown and firm to the touch. Transfer to a wire rack and leave to cool.

4 To make the frosting, put the butter in a bowl and beat until fluffy. Sift in the icing sugar and beat together until well mixed, gradually beating in the milk.

5 To decorate the cupcakes, using a piping bag fitted with a large star nozzle, pipe the frosting on top of each cupcake, then add a glacé, maraschino or fresh cherry to decorate.

almond & apricot spice cupcakes

MAKES 30

175 g/6 oz plain flour

1 tbsp baking powder

1 tsp ground allspice

175 g/6 oz unsalted butter, softened

175 g/6 oz golden caster sugar

3 eggs, beaten

1 tsp almond extract

2 tbsp milk

85 g/3 oz ready-to-eat dried apricots, finely chopped

40 g/1½ oz ground almonds

150 g/5½ oz dulce de leche

25 g/1 oz flaked almonds, toasted

1 Preheat the oven to 190°C/375°F/Gas Mark 5. Put 30 paper cases into bun tins or put 30 double-layer paper cases onto baking trays.

2 Sift the flour, baking powder and allspice into a large bowl and add the butter, sugar, eggs and almond extract. Beat well until the mixture is smooth, then stir in the milk, apricots and ground almonds. Spoon the mixture into the paper cases.

3 Bake in the preheated oven for 15–20 minutes, or until golden brown and firm to the touch. Transfer the cupcakes to a wire rack and leave to cool.

4 Spoon about a teaspoonful of dulce de leche on top of each cupcake and top with the flaked almonds.

pistachio cupcakes

MAKES 16

85 g/3 oz unsalted pistachio nuts

115 g/4oz butter, softened

140 g/5 oz golden caster sugar

140 g/5 oz self-raising flour, sifted

2 eggs, lightly beaten

4 tbsp Greek-style yogurt

frosting

115 g/4 oz butter, softened

2 tbsp lime juice cordial

few drops green food colouring (optional)

200 g/7 oz icing sugar

1 tbsp pistachio nuts, chopped

1 Preheat the oven to 180°C/350°F/Gas Mark 4. Put 16 paper baking cases in 2 bun trays or put 16 double-layer paper cases on a baking tray.

2 Put the pistachio nuts in a food processor or blender and process for a few seconds until finely ground. Add the butter, sugar, flour, eggs and yogurt and then process until evenly mixed. Spoon the mixture into the paper cases.

3 Bake the cupcakes in the preheated oven for 20–25 minutes or until golden brown and firm to the touch. Transfer to a wire rack and leave to cool.

4 To make the frosting, put the butter, lime cordial and food colouring (if using) in a bowl and beat until fluffy. Sift in the icing sugar and beat until smooth. Swirl the icing over the cupcakes and sprinkle with the chopped pistachio nuts.

banana & pecan cupcakes

MAKES 24

225 g/8 oz plain flour

1¼ tsp baking powder

¼ tsp bicarbonate of soda

2 ripe bananas

115 g/4 oz butter, softened

115 g/4 oz caster sugar

½ tsp vanilla extract

2 eggs, lightly beaten

4 tbsp soured cream

55 g/2 oz pecan nuts, roughly chopped

frosting

115 g/4 oz butter, softened

175 g/6 oz icing sugar

25 g/1 oz pecan nuts, finely chopped

1 Preheat the oven to 190°C/375°/Gas Mark 5. Put 24 paper baking cases into bun tins or put 24 double-layer cases onto baking trays.

2 Sift together the flour, baking powder and bicarbonate of soda. Peel the bananas, put them in a bowl and mash with a fork. Put the butter, sugar and vanilla in a bowl and beat together until light and fluffy. Gradually add the eggs, beating well after each addition. Stir in the mashed bananas and soured cream. Using a metal spoon, fold in the sifted flour mixture and chopped nuts, then spoon the mixture into the paper cases.

3 Bake in the preheated oven for 20 minutes, or until golden brown and firm to the touch. Transfer the cupcakes to a wire rack and leave to cool.

4 To make the frosting, put the butter in a bowl and beat until fluffy. Sift in the icing sugar and mix together well. Spread the icing on top of the cupcakes and sprinkle with the finely chopped pecans before serving.

macadamia & maple cupcakes

MAKES 10

85 g/3 oz butter, softened

55 g/2 oz light soft brown sugar

2 tbsp maple syrup

1 large egg, lightly beaten

55 g/2 oz macadamia nuts, chopped

85 g/3 oz self-raising flour

1 tbsp milk

2 tbsp chopped macadamia nuts, lightly toasted

frosting

25 g/1 oz butter, softened

2 tbsp maple syrup

85 g/3 oz icing sugar, sifted

85 g/3 oz cream cheese

1 Preheat the oven to 190°C/375°F/Gas Mark 5. Put 10 paper baking cases in a bun tray or put 10 double-layer paper cases on a baking tray.

2 Put the butter, sugar and maple syrup in a bowl and beat together until light and fluffy. Gradually beat in the egg. Sift in the flour and, using a metal spoon, fold into the mixture with the nuts and milk. Spoon the mixture into the paper cases.

3 Bake the cupcakes in the preheated oven for 20 minutes or until golden brown and firm to the touch. Transfer to a wire rack and leave to cool.

4 To make the frosting, beat the butter and maple syrup together until smooth. Fold in the icing sugar and beat in thoroughly. Gently beat in the cream cheese. Swirl the icing on the top of the cupcakes and sprinkle over the toasted nuts.

pure indulgence almond cupcakes

MAKES 12

100 g/3½ oz butter, softened

100 g/3½ oz caster sugar

2 eggs, lightly beaten

¼ tsp almond extract

4 tbsp single cream

175 g/6 oz plain flour

1½ tsp baking powder

70 g/2½ oz ground almonds

topping

115 g/4 oz butter, softened

225 g/8 oz icing sugar

few drops of almond extract

25 g/1 oz toasted flaked almonds

1 Preheat the oven to 180°C/350°/Gas Mark 4. Put 12 paper baking cases into bun tins or put 12 double-layer cases onto baking trays.

2 Place the butter and sugar in a large bowl and beat together until light and fluffy. Gradually beat in the eggs, then add the almond extract and cream. Sift in the flour and baking powder and fold into the mixture, then fold in the ground almonds. Spoon the mixture into the paper cases.

3 Bake in the preheated oven for 25 minutes, or until golden brown and firm to the touch. Transfer the cupcakes to a wire rack and leave to cool.

4 To make the icing, place the butter in a large bowl and beat until creamy. Sift in the icing sugar. Add the almond extract and beat together until smooth. Spread the icing on top of each cake, using a knife to form the icing into swirls. Sprinkle the flaked almonds over the top.

sticky date & toffee cupcakes

MAKES 6

85 g/3 oz dried stoned dates, chopped

½ tsp bicarbonate of soda

100 ml/3½ fl oz water

85 g/3 oz butter, softened, plus extra for greasing

85 g/3 oz soft dark brown sugar

1 tsp vanilla extract

2 eggs, lightly beaten

115 g/4 oz self-raising flour

double cream, to serve

toffee sauce

85 g/3 oz soft dark brown sugar

55 g/2 oz butter

4 tbsp double cream

1 Put the dates, bicarbonate of soda and water in a small saucepan and bring to the boil. Remove from the heat and set aside to cool.

2 Preheat the oven to 180°C/350°F/Gas Mark 4. Grease six 150-ml/5-fl oz ovenproof teacups or dishes (such as ramekins) with butter.

3 Put the butter, sugar and vanilla extract in a bowl and beat together until light and fluffy. Gradually beat in the eggs. Sift in the flour and, using a metal spoon, fold into the mixture followed by the date mixture. Spoon the mixture into the cups or dishes.

4 Put the cups or dishes on a baking sheet and bake in the preheated oven for 20–25 minutes or until risen and firm to the touch.

5 To make the toffee sauce, put all the ingredients in a small saucepan and heat until the butter has melted. Simmer for 5 minutes, stirring occasionally. Using a skewer, prick a few holes in each warm cupcake and drizzle over some of the sauce. Serve the cupcakes with the rest of the toffee sauce and the double cream.

moist walnut cupcakes

MAKES 12

85 g/3 oz walnuts

55 g/2 oz butter, softened

100 g/3½ oz caster sugar

grated rind of ½ lemon

70 g/2½ oz self-raising flour, sifted

2 eggs

12 walnut halves, to decorate

frosting

55 g/2 oz butter, softened

85 g/3 oz icing sugar

grated rind of ½ lemon

1 tsp lemon juice

1 Preheat the oven to 190°C/375°F/Gas Mark 5. Put 12 paper baking cases in a bun tray, or put 12 double-layer paper cases on a baking tray.

2 Put the walnuts in a food processor and, using a pulsating action, blend until finely ground, being careful not to over-grind, which will turn them to oil. Add the butter, cut into small pieces, along with the sugar, lemon rind, flour and eggs, then blend until evenly mixed. Spoon the mixture into the paper cases.

3 Bake the cupcakes in the preheated oven for 20 minutes, or until well risen and golden brown. Transfer to a wire rack and leave to cool.

4 To make the icing, put the butter in a bowl and beat until fluffy. Sift in the icing sugar, add the lemon rind and juice and mix well together.

5 When the cupcakes are cold, spread some of the icing on top of each cupcake and top with a walnut half to decorate.

VARIATION

Replace the walnuts with pecan nuts and the lemon rind and juice with orange rind and juice to make moist pecan cupcakes.

4

Superbly
Special

coffee fudge cupcakes

MAKES 28

175 g/6 oz plain white flour

1 tbsp baking powder

175 g/6 oz unsalted butter, softened

175 g/6 oz caster sugar

3 eggs, beaten

1 tsp coffee extract

2 tbsp milk

chocolate-covered coffee beans, to decorate

frosting

55 g/2 oz unsalted butter

115 g/4 oz light muscovado sugar

2 tbsp single cream or milk

½ tsp coffee extract

400 g/14 oz icing sugar, sifted

1 Preheat the oven to 190°C/375°F/Gas Mark 5. Put 28 paper cases into bun tins or put 28 double-layer paper cases onto baking trays.

2 Sift the flour and baking powder into a large bowl and add the butter, caster sugar, eggs and coffee extract. Beat well until the mixture is smooth, then beat in the milk. Spoon the mixture into the paper cases.

3 Bake the cupcakes in the preheated oven for 15–20 minutes, or until golden brown and firm to the touch. Transfer to a wire rack and leave to cool.

4 For the frosting, place the butter, muscovado sugar, cream and coffee extract in a saucepan over a medium heat and stir until melted and smooth. Bring to the boil and boil, stirring, for 2 minutes. Remove from the heat and beat in the icing sugar.

5 Stir the frosting until smooth and thick, then spoon into a piping bag fitted with a large star nozzle. Pipe a swirl of frosting on top of each cupcake and top with a coffee bean.

marzipan flower cupcakes

MAKES 12

115 g/4 oz self-raising flour

½ tsp baking powder

115 g/4 oz soft tub margarine

115 g/4 oz caster sugar, sifted

2 eggs, lightly beaten

few drops almond extract

topping

200 g/7 oz marzipan

icing sugar, for dusting

2 tbsp apricot jam

1 Preheat the oven to 180°C/350°F/Gas Mark 4. Put 12 paper baking cases in a bun tray or put 12 double-layer paper cases on a baking tray.

2 Sift the flour and baking powder into a bowl. Add the margarine, sugar, eggs and almond extract and, using an electric hand whisk, beat together until smooth. Spoon the mixture into the paper cases.

3 Bake the cupcakes in the preheated oven for 20 minutes or until golden brown and firm to the touch. Transfer to a wire rack and leave to cool.

4 To top the cupcakes, roll out the marzipan on a surface dusted lightly with sifted icing sugar. Using a 3-cm/1¼-inch round cutter, stamp out 60 circles, re-rolling the marzipan as necessary. Spread a little apricot jam over the top of each cupcake. Pinch the marzipan circles at one side to create petal shapes and arrange five petals on top of each cupcake. Roll small balls of remaining marzipan for the flower centres and place in the middle of the cupcakes.

apple pie cupcakes

MAKES 12

50 g/1¾ oz butter, softened

70 g/2½ oz demerara sugar

1 egg, lightly beaten

150 g/5½ oz plain flour

1½ tsp baking powder

½ tsp ground mixed spice

1 large cooking apple, peeled, cored and finely chopped

1 tbsp orange juice

topping

40 g/ 1½ oz plain flour

½ tsp ground mixed spice

25 g/1 oz butter

40 g/1½ oz caster sugar

1 Preheat the oven to 180°C/350°F/Gas Mark 4. Put 12 paper baking cases into bun tins or put 12 double-layer cases onto baking trays.

2 To make the topping, place the flour, mixed spice, butter and sugar in a large bowl and rub in with your fingertips until the mixture resembles fine breadcrumbs. Set aside.

3 Place the butter and sugar in a large bowl and beat together until light and fluffy, then gradually beat in the egg. Sift in the flour, baking powder and mixed spice and fold into the mixture, then fold in the chopped apple and orange juice. Spoon the mixture into the paper cases. Add the topping to cover the top of each cupcake and press down gently.

4 Bake the cupcakes in the preheated oven for 30 minutes, or until golden brown. Leave the cupcakes to cool in the tin for 2–3 minutes and serve warm, or leave to cool for 10 minutes and then transfer to a wire rack to cool completely.

birthday party cupcakes

MAKES 24

225 g/8 oz soft tub margarine

225 g/8 oz caster sugar

4 eggs

225 g/8 oz self-raising flour, sifted

a variety of small sweets and chocolates, sugar-coated chocolates, dried fruits, edible sugar flower shapes, cake decorating sprinkles, sugar strands, and hundreds and thousands

candles and candleholders (optional)

frosting

175 g/6 oz butter, softened

350 g/12 oz icing sugar

1 Preheat the oven to 180°C/350°F/Gas Mark 4. Put 24 paper baking cases in 2 bun trays, or put 24 double-layer paper cases on 2 baking trays.

2 Put the margarine, sugar, eggs and flour in a large bowl and, using an electric hand whisk, beat together until just smooth. Spoon the mixture into the paper cases.

3 Bake the cupcakes in the preheated oven for 15–20 minutes, or until well risen, golden brown and firm to the touch. Transfer to a wire rack and leave to cool.

4 To make the frosting, put the butter in a bowl and beat until fluffy. Sift in the icing sugar and beat together until smooth and creamy. Put the frosting in a piping bag, fitted with a large star-shaped nozzle. When the cupcakes are cold, pipe circles of frosting on top of each cupcake, then decorate to your choice. If desired, place a candle in the top of each.

christmas cupcakes

MAKES 16

125 g/4½ oz butter, softened

200 g/7 oz caster sugar

4–6 drops almond extract

4 eggs, lightly beaten

150 g/5½ oz self-raising flour, sifted

175 g/6 oz ground almonds

topping

450 g/1 lb white ready-to-roll fondant icing

icing sugar, for dusting

55 g/2 oz green ready-to-roll coloured fondant icing

25 g/1 oz red ready-to-roll coloured fondant icing

1 Preheat the oven to 180°C/350°F/Gas Mark 4. Put 16 paper muffin cases in a muffin tray.

2 Put the butter, sugar and almond extract in a bowl and beat together until light and fluffy. Gradually add the eggs, beating well after each addition. Add the flour and fold it into the mixture, then fold in the ground almonds. Spoon the mixture into the paper cases to half-fill them.

3 Bake the cakes in the preheated oven for 20 minutes, or until well risen, golden brown and firm to the touch. Transfer to a wire rack and leave to cool.

4 When the cakes are cold, knead the white icing until pliable, then roll out on a surface lightly dusted with, sifted icing sugar. Using a 7-cm/2¾-inch plain round cutter, cut out 16 circles, re-rolling as necessary. Place a circle on top of each cupcake.

5 Roll out the green icing on a surface lightly dusted with sifted icing sugar. Rub icing sugar into the icing to prevent it from spotting. Using a holly-leaf-shaped cutter, cut out 32 leaves, re-rolling the icing as necessary. Brush each leaf with a little cooled boiled water and place 2 leaves on top of each cupcake. Roll the red icing to form 48 berries and place in the centre of the leaves, to decorate.

festive cupcakes

MAKES 14

115 g/4 oz mixed dried fruit

1 tsp finely grated orange rind

2 tbsp brandy or orange juice

85 g/3 oz butter, softened

85 g/3 oz light soft brown sugar

1 large egg, lightly beaten

115 g/4 oz self-raising flour

1 tsp ground mixed spice

1 tbsp silver dragées (cake decoration balls), to decorate

icing

85 g/3 oz icing sugar

2 tbsp orange juice

1 Put the mixed fruit, orange rind and brandy in a small bowl. Cover and leave to soak for 1 hour.

2 Preheat the oven to 190°C/375°F/Gas Mark 5. Put 14 paper baking cases in 2 bun trays or put 14 double-layer paper cases on a baking tray.

3 Put the butter and sugar in a mixing bowl and beat together until light and fluffy. Gradually beat in the egg. Sift in the flour and mixed spice and, using a metal spoon, fold them into the mixture followed by the soaked fruit. Spoon the mixture into the paper cases.

4 Bake the cupcakes in the preheated oven for 15–20 minutes or until golden brown and firm to the touch. Transfer to a cooling rack and leave to cool.

5 To make the icing, sift the icing sugar into a bowl and gradually mix in enough orange juice until the mixture is smooth and thick enough to coat the back of a wooden spoon. Using a teaspoon, drizzle the icing in a zig-zag pattern over the cupcakes. Decorate with the silver dragées. Leave to set.

valentine heart cupcakes

MAKES 6

85 g/3 oz butter, softened

85 g/3 oz caster sugar

½ tsp vanilla extract

2 eggs, lightly beaten

70 g/2½ oz plain flour

1 tbsp cocoa powder

1 tsp baking powder

6 pink edible sugar flowers, to decorate

marzipan hearts

35 g/1¼ oz marzipan

red food colouring (liquid or paste)

icing sugar, for dusting

frosting

55 g/2 oz butter, softened

115 g/4 oz icing sugar

25 g/1 oz plain chocolate, melted

1 To make the hearts, knead the marzipan until pliable, then add a few drops of red colouring and knead until evenly coloured. Roll out the marzipan to a thickness of 5 mm/¼ inch on a surface dusted with icing sugar. Using a small heart-shaped cutter, cut out 6 hearts. Place these on a tray, lined with greaseproof paper and dusted with sifted icing sugar, and leave to dry for 3–4 hours.

2 To make the cupcakes, preheat the oven to 180°C/350°F/ Gas Mark 4. Put six paper muffin cases in a muffin tin.

3 Put the butter, sugar and vanilla extract in a bowl and beat together until light and fluffy. Gradually add the eggs, beating well after each addition. Sift in the flour, cocoa powder and baking powder and, using a large metal spoon, fold into the mixture. Spoon the mixture into the paper cases.

4 Bake the cupcakes in the preheated oven for 20–25 minutes, or until well risen and firm to the touch. Transfer to a wire rack and leave to cool.

5 To make the frosting, put the butter in a large bowl and beat until fluffy. Sift in the icing sugar and beat together until smooth. Add the melted chocolate and beat together until well mixed. When the cupcakes are cold, spread some of the frosting on top of each cupcake and decorate with a marzipan heart and sugar flower.

easter cupcakes

MAKES 12

115 g/4 oz butter, softened

115 g/4 oz caster sugar

2 eggs, lightly beaten

85 g/3 oz self-raising flour

25 g/1 oz cocoa powder

two 130 g/4¾ oz packets mini chocolate candy shell eggs

frosting

85 g/3 oz butter, softened

175 g/6 oz icing sugar

1 tbsp milk

2–3 drops of vanilla extract

1 Preheat the oven to 180°C/350°F/Gas Mark 4. Put 12 paper baking cases in a bun tray, or put 12 double-layer paper cases on a baking tray.

2 Put the butter and sugar in a bowl and beat together until light and fluffy. Gradually add the eggs, beating well after each addition. Sift in the flour and cocoa powder and, using a large metal spoon, fold into the mixture. Spoon the mixture into the paper cases.

3 Bake the cupcakes in the preheated oven for 15–20 minutes, or until well risen and firm to the touch. Transfer to a wire rack and leave to cool.

4 To make the frosting, put the butter in a bowl and beat until fluffy. Sift in the icing sugar and beat together until well mixed, adding the milk and vanilla extract. Put the frosting in a piping bag fitted with a large star-shaped nozzle. When the cupcakes are cold, pipe circles of frosting on top of the cupcakes to form nests. Decorate with chocolate eggs.

halloween cupcakes

MAKES 12

115 g/4 oz soft tub margarine

115 g/4 oz caster sugar

2 eggs

115 g/4 oz self-raising flour, sifted

topping

200 g/7 oz orange ready-to-roll coloured fondant icing

icing sugar, for dusting

55 g/2 oz black ready-to-roll coloured fondant icing

black cake-writing icing

yellow cake-writing icing

1 Preheat the oven to 180°C/350°F/Gas Mark 4. Put 12 paper baking cases in a bun tray, or put 12 double-layer paper cases on a baking tray.

2 Put the margarine, sugar, eggs and flour in a bowl and, using an electric hand whisk, beat together until smooth. Spoon the mixture into the cases.

3 Bake the cupcakes in the preheated oven for 15–20 minutes, or until well risen, golden brown and firm to the touch. Transfer to a wire rack and leave to cool.

4 When the cupcakes are cold, knead the orange icing until pliable, then roll out on a surface lightly dusted with sifted icing sugar. Using the palm of your hand, lightly rub sifted icing sugar into the icing to prevent it from spotting. Using a 5.5-cm/2¼-inch plain round cutter, cut out 12 circles, re-rolling the icing as necessary. Place a circle on top of each cupcake.

5 Roll out the black icing on a surface lightly dusted with icing sugar. Using the palm of your hand, lightly rub icing sugar into the icing to prevent it from spotting. Using a 3-cm/1¼-inch plain round cutter, cut out 12 circles and place them on the centre of the cupcakes. Using black writing icing, pipe 8 legs on to each spider and using yellow writing icing, draw 2 eyes and a mouth.

baby shower cupcakes

MAKES 24

225 g/8 oz butter, softened

225 g/8 oz caster sugar

finely grated rind of 2 lemons

4 eggs, lightly beaten

225 g/8 oz self-raising flour, sifted

24 sugared almonds

icing

350 g/12 oz icing sugar

red or blue food colouring (liquid or paste)

1 Preheat the oven to 180°C/350°F/Gas Mark 4. Put 24 paper muffin cases in muffin tins.

2 Put the butter, sugar and lemon rind in a bowl and beat together until light and fluffy. Gradually add the eggs, beating well after each addition. Add the flour and, using a large metal spoon, fold into the mixture. Spoon the mixture into the paper cases to half fill them.

3 Bake the cupcakes in the preheated oven for 20–25 minutes, or until well risen, golden brown and firm to the touch. Transfer to a wire rack and leave to cool.

4 When the cakes are cold, make the icing. Sift the icing sugar into a bowl. Add 6–8 teaspoons of hot water and stir until the mixture is smooth and thick enough to coat the back of a wooden spoon. Dip a skewer into the red or blue food colouring, then stir it into the icing until it is evenly coloured, pink or pale blue.

5 Spoon some icing on top of each cupcake. Top each with a sugared almond and leave to set for about 30 minutes, before serving.

gold star cupcakes

MAKES 12

MAKES 12

85 g/3 oz butter, softened

85 g/3 oz light soft brown sugar

1 large egg, beaten

85 g/3 oz self-raising flour

½ tsp ground cinnamon

1 tbsp milk

gold stars

85 g/3 oz yellow ready-to-roll coloured fondant icing

icing sugar, for dusting

edible gold dusting powder (optional)

icing

85 g/3 oz icing sugar

2–3 tsp lemon juice

1 Preheat the oven to 180°C/350°F/Gas Mark 4. Put 12 paper baking cases in a bun tray or put 12 double-layer paper cases on a baking tray.

2 Put the butter and sugar in a mixing bowl and beat together until light and fluffy. Gradually beat in the egg. Sift in the flour and cinnamon and, using a metal spoon, fold them into the mixture with the milk. Spoon the mixture into the paper cases.

3 Bake the cupcakes in the preheated oven for 20 minutes or until golden brown and firm to the touch. Transfer to a wire rack and leave to cool.

4 To make the gold stars, roll the yellow fondant icing out on a surface lightly dusted with sifted icing sugar and, using a small star cutter, stamp out 12 stars. Brush each star with a little gold dusting powder, if using. Set aside on a sheet of baking parchment.

5 To make the icing, sift the icing sugar into a bowl and stir in enough lemon juice to make a smooth and thick icing.

6 Spoon the icing on top of the cupcakes and top each with a gold star. Leave to set.

anniversary cupcakes

MAKES 24

225 g/8 oz butter, softened

225 g/8 oz caster sugar

1 tsp vanilla extract

4 large eggs, lightly beaten

225 g/8 oz self-raising flour, sifted

5 tbsp milk

frosting

175 g/6 oz unsalted butter

350 g/12 oz icing sugar

25 g/1 oz silver or gold dragées (cake decoration balls)

1 Preheat the oven to 180°C/350°F/Gas Mark 4. Put 24 silver or gold foil cake cases in bun trays, or arrange them on baking trays.

2 Put the butter, sugar and vanilla extract in a bowl and beat together until light and fluffy. Gradually add the eggs, beating well after each addition. Add the flour and, using a large metal spoon, fold into the mixture with the milk. Spoon the mixture into the paper cases.

3 Bake the cupcakes in the preheated oven for 15–20 minutes, or until well risen and firm to the touch. Transfer to a wire rack and leave to cool.

4 To make the frosting, put the butter in a bowl and beat until fluffy. Sift in the icing sugar and beat together. Put the frosting in a piping bag, fitted with a star-shaped nozzle.

5 When the cupcakes are cold, pipe circles of frosting on top of each cupcake to cover the tops. Sprinkle over the silver or gold dragées before serving.

cherry cupcakes

MAKES 28

175 g/6 oz plain flour, sifted

70 g/2½ oz glacé cherries, chopped

1 tbsp baking powder

1 tbsp cornflour

175 g/6 oz unsalted butter, softened

175 g/6 oz caster sugar

3 eggs, beaten

1 tsp vanilla extract

14 glacé cherries, halved, to decorate

frosting

250 g/9 oz ricotta cheese

70 g/2½ oz icing sugar, sifted

½ tsp vanilla extract

1 Preheat the oven to 190°C/375°F/Gas Mark 5. Put 28 paper cases in a bun tray, or put 28 double-layer paper cases on baking trays.

2 Stir a tablespoon of the flour into the chopped glacé cherries. Sift the remaining flour with the baking powder and cornflour into a large bowl and add the butter, caster sugar, eggs and vanilla extract. Beat well until the mixture is smooth, then stir in the glacé cherry and flour mixture. Spoon the mixture into the paper cases.

3 Bake the cupcakes in the preheated oven for 15–20 minutes, or until golden brown and firm to the touch. Transfer the cupcakes to a wire rack and leave to cool.

4 To make the frosting, mix the ricotta with icing sugar and vanilla extract, then spoon a little on top of each cupcake. Top each with half a glacé cherry.

vanilla hazelnut yogurt cupcakes

MAKES 26

175 g/6 oz plain flour

2 tsp cornflour

1 tbsp baking powder

175 g/6 oz natural yogurt

175 g/6 oz golden caster sugar

3 eggs, beaten

1 tsp vanilla extract

40 g/1½ oz hazelnuts, finely chopped

topping

100 g/3½ oz icing sugar, sifted

40 g/1½ oz natural yogurt

25 g/1 oz hazelnuts, roughly chopped

1 Preheat the oven to 190°C/375°F/Gas Mark 5. Put 26 paper cases in a bun tray, or put 26 double-layer paper cases on baking trays.

2 Sift the flour, cornflour and baking powder into a large bowl and add the yogurt, caster sugar, eggs and vanilla extract. Beat well until the mixture is smooth, then stir in the finely chopped hazelnuts.

3 Divide the mixture between the paper cases. Bake in the preheated oven for 15–20 minutes, or until risen, firm and golden brown. Transfer the cupcakes to a wire rack to cool.

4 For the topping, mix the icing sugar and yogurt until smooth, then drizzle over the cupcakes. Scatter over the roughly chopped hazelnuts. Leave to set.

orange saffron mini cupcakes

MAKES 90

2–3 tbsp orange juice

pinch of saffron threads

175 g/6 oz plain white flour

1 tbsp baking powder

175 g/6 oz unsalted butter, softened

175 g/6 oz golden caster sugar

3 eggs, beaten

finely grated rind of 1 orange

150 g/5½ oz icing sugar, sifted

fine strips of orange zest, to decorate

1 Preheat the oven to 190°C/375°F/Gas Mark 5. Arrange 90 mini paper cases on 2–3 baking sheets.

2 Heat 2 tablespoons of the orange juice with the saffron threads until almost boiling, then remove from the heat and leave to stand for 10 minutes.

3 Sift the flour and baking powder into a large bowl and add the butter, caster sugar and eggs. Beat well until the mixture is smooth, then stir in the orange rind and half the saffron and orange juice mixture. Spoon the mixture into the paper cases.

4 Bake the cupcakes in the preheated oven for 12–15 minutes, or until golden brown and firm to the touch. Transfer the cupcakes to a wire rack and leave to cool.

5 Mix the remaining saffron and orange juice mixture with the icing sugar to make a smooth paste, adding a little extra orange juice if needed. Spoon a little on top of each cupcake, decorate with strips of orange zest and leave to set.

tiramisu cupcakes

MAKES 12

115 g/4 oz unsalted butter

115 g/4 oz soft light brown sugar

2 eggs, beaten

115 g/4 oz self-raising flour, sifted

½ tsp baking powder

2 tsp coffee granules

25 g/1 oz icing sugar

4 tbsp water

2 tbsp finely grated plain chocolate, for dusting

frosting

225 g/8 oz mascarpone cheese

85 g/3 oz caster sugar

2 tbsp masala or sweet sherry

1 Preheat the oven to 180°C/350°F/Gas Mark 4. Put 12 paper baking cases in a bun tray or put 12 double-layer cases on a baking tray.

2 Place the butter, sugar, eggs, flour and baking powder in a bowl and, using an electric whisk, beat together until smooth and creamy. Spoon the mixture into the paper cases.

3 Bake the cupcakes in the preheated oven for 15–20 minutes until risen, golden and firm to the touch.

4 Place the coffee granules, icing sugar and water in a pan and heat gently, stirring until the coffee and sugar have dissolved. Boil for 1 minute then leave to cool for 10 minutes. Brush the coffee syrup over the top of the warm cupcakes. Transfer the cupcakes to a wire rack and leave to cool.

5 For the frosting, put the mascarpone, sugar and marsala in a bowl and beat together until smooth. Spread over the top of the cakes. Using a star template sprinkle the grated chocolate over the frosting.

banoffee cupcakes

MAKES 4

100 g/3½ oz butter, softened, plus extra for greasing

100 g/3½ oz soft light brown sugar

2 eggs, lightly beaten

100 g/3½ oz self–raising flour

1 small ripe banana, peeled and mashed

topping

150 ml/5 fl oz double cream

½ banana, peeled and sliced

2 tbsp dulce de leche (toffee sauce)

1 tbsp grated chocolate

1 Preheat the oven to 190°C/375°F/Gas Mark 5. Grease four 200-ml/7-fl oz ovenproof teacups or dishes (such as ramekins) with butter.

2 Put the butter and sugar in a bowl and beat together until light and fluffy. Gradually beat in the eggs. Sift in the flour and, using a metal spoon, fold into the mixture with the mashed banana. Spoon the mixture into the cups or dishes.

3 Put the cups or dishes on a baking sheet and bake in the preheated oven for 20–25 minutes or until risen and golden brown. Leave to cool.

4 To make the topping, whisk the cream in a bowl until softly peaking. Spoon the whipped cream on top of each cupcake then arrange 3–4 banana slices on top. Drizzle over the dulce de leche and sprinkle over the grated chocolate. Store the cupcakes in the refrigerator until ready to serve.

raspberry ripple cupcakes

MAKES 32

175 g/6 oz plain white flour

1 tbsp baking powder

1 tbsp cornflour

175 g/6 oz unsalted butter, softened

175 g/6 oz caster sugar

3 eggs, beaten

1 tsp almond extract

200 g/7 oz fresh raspberries

vanilla sugar, for sprinkling

1 Preheat the oven to 190°C/375°F/Gas Mark 5. Put 32 paper cases in bun trays or put 32 double-layer paper cases on baking trays.

2 Sift the flour, baking powder and cornflour into a large bowl and add the butter, caster sugar, eggs and almond extract. Beat well until the mixture is smooth. Mash the raspberries lightly with a fork, then fold into the mixture. Spoon the mixture into the paper cases.

3 Bake the cupcakes in the preheated oven for 15–20 minutes, or until golden brown and firm to the touch. Transfer the cupcakes to a wire rack and leave to cool.

4 Sprinkle with vanilla sugar before serving.

cream tea cupcakes

MAKES 10

85 g/3 oz unsalted butter, softened

85 g/3oz caster sugar

½ tsp vanilla extract

1 large egg, lightly beaten

85 g/3 oz self-raising flour

1 tbsp milk

40 g/1½ oz raisins

115 g/4 oz small strawberries, hulled and sliced

1 tbsp strawberry jam

115 g/4 oz clotted cream

icing sugar, for dusting

1 Preheat the oven to 190°C/375°F/Gas Mark 5. Put 10 paper baking cases in a bun tray or put 10 double-layer paper cases on a baking tray.

2 Put the butter, sugar and vanilla extract in a mixing bowl and beat together until light and fluffy. Gradually beat in the egg. Sift in the flour and, using a metal spoon, fold into the mixture with the milk and raisins. Spoon the mixture into the paper cases.

3 Bake the cupcakes in the preheated oven for 15–20 minutes or until golden brown and firm to the touch. Transfer to a wire rack and leave to cool.

4 When the cupcakes are cold, use a serrated knife to cut a circle from the top of each cupcake. Gently mix the strawberries and jam together and divide between the cupcakes. Top each with a small dollop of clotted cream. Replace the cake tops and dust with sifted icing sugar. Store the cupcakes in the refrigerator until ready to serve.

feather-iced coffee cupcakes

MAKES 16

115 g/4 oz butter, softened

115 g/4 oz soft light brown sugar

2 eggs

115 g/4 oz self-raising flour

½ tsp baking powder

1 tbsp instant coffee granules dissolved in 1 tbsp boiling water and cooled

2 tbsp soured cream

icing

225 g/8 oz icing sugar

4 tsp warm water

1 tbsp instant coffee granules dissolved in 2 tbsp boiling water

1 Preheat the oven to 190°C/375°F/Gas Mark 5. Put 16 paper baking cases in 2 bun trays, or put 16 double-layer paper cases on a baking tray.

2 Put the butter, sugar and eggs in a bowl. Sift in the flour and baking powder, then beat together until smooth. Add the dissolved coffee and soured cream and beat together until well mixed. Spoon the mixture into the paper cases.

3 Bake the cupcakes in the preheated oven for 20 minutes, or until well risen and golden brown. Transfer to a wire rack and leave to cool.

4 To make the icing, sift 85 g/3 oz of the icing sugar into a bowl, then gradually mix in the water. Sift the remaining icing sugar into a bowl, then stir in the dissolved coffee. Put the coffee icing in a piping bag, fitted with a piping nozzle. When the cupcakes are cold, coat the tops of the cupcakes with the white icing and pipe the coffee icing across in parallel lines. Draw a skewer across the piped lines in both directions.

lemon meringue cupcakes

MAKES 4

85 g/3 oz butter, softened plus extra for greasing

85 g/3 oz caster sugar

finely grated rind and juice from ½ lemon

1 large egg, lightly beaten

85 g/3 oz self-raising flour

2 tbsp lemon curd

meringue

2 egg whites

115 g/4 oz caster sugar

1 Preheat the oven to 190°C/375°F/Gas Mark 5. Grease four 200-ml/7-fl oz ovenproof teacups or dishes (such as ramekins) with butter.

2 Put the butter, sugar and lemon rind in a bowl and beat together until light and fluffy. Gradually beat in the egg. Sift in the flour and, using a metal spoon, fold into the mixture with the lemon juice. Spoon the mixture into the cups or dishes.

3 Put the cups or dishes on a baking sheet and bake in the preheated oven for 15 minutes or until risen and pale golden brown.

4 Whilst the cupcakes are baking, make the meringue by putting the egg whites in a clean grease free bowl and, using a hand held electric whisk, whisk until stiff. Gradually whisk in the caster sugar to form a stiff and glossy meringue.

5 Spread the lemon curd over the hot cupcakes then swirl over the meringue. Return the cupcakes to the oven for 4–5 minutes until the meringue is golden. Serve immediately.

toffee apple cupcakes

MAKES 16

**55 g/2 oz butter,
plus extra for greasing**

2 apples

1 tbsp lemon juice

250 g/9 oz plain flour

2 tsp baking powder

1½ tsp ground cinnamon

**70 g/2½ oz light muscovado
sugar**

100 ml/3½ fl oz milk

100 ml/3½ fl oz apple juice

1 egg, beaten

toffee topping

2 tbsp single cream

**40 g/1½ oz light muscovado
sugar**

15 g/½ oz unsalted butter

1 Preheat the oven to 200°C/400°F/Gas Mark 6. Grease 16 cups of two 12-cup bun trays with butter.

2 Core and roughly grate one of the apples. Slice the remaining apple into 5 mm/¼ inch thick wedges and toss in the lemon juice. Sift together the flour, baking powder and cinnamon, then stir in the sugar and grated apple.

3 Melt the butter and mix with the milk, apple juice and egg. Stir the liquid mixture into the dry ingredients, mixing lightly until just combined. Spoon the mixture into the paper cases and arrange two apple slices on top of each.

4 Bake in the preheated oven for 15–20 minutes or until risen, firm and golden brown. Transfer to a wire rack and leave to cool.

5 For the toffee topping, place all the ingredients in a small pan and heat, stirring, until the sugar is dissolved. Increase the heat and boil rapidly for 2 minutes, or until slightly thickened and syrupy. Cool slightly, then drizzle over the cakes and leave to set.

honey & spice cupcakes

MAKES 22

140 g/5 oz unsalted butter

100 g/3½ oz light muscovado sugar

100 g/3½ oz honey

200 g/7 oz self-raising flour

1 tsp ground allspice

2 eggs, beaten

22 whole blanched almonds

1 Preheat the oven to 180°C/350°F/Gas Mark 4. Put 22 paper baking cases into bun tins or put 22 double-layer cases onto baking trays.

2 Place the butter, sugar and honey in a large saucepan and heat gently, stirring, until the butter is melted and the sugar has dissolved. Remove the pan from the heat.

3 Sift together the flour and allspice and stir into the mixture in the saucepan, then beat in the eggs, mixing to a smooth batter. Spoon the batter into the paper cases and place an almond of top of each one.

4 Bake in the preheated oven for 20–25 minutes, or until well risen and golden brown. Transfer to a wire rack to cool.

24-carrot gold cupcakes

MAKES 12

175 g/6 oz butter, softened, or soft margarine

115 g/4 oz golden caster sugar

2 eggs, lightly beaten

300 g/10 oz carrots, peeled and grated

55 g/2 oz walnuts, finely chopped

2 tbsp orange juice

grated rind of ½ orange

175 g/6 oz self-raising flour

1 tsp ground cinnamon

12 walnut halves, to decorate

frosting

115 g/4 oz full-fat cream cheese

225 g/8 oz icing sugar, sifted

1 tbsp orange juice

1 Preheat the oven to 180°C/350°F/Gas Mark 4. Put 12 paper cases in a bun tray, or put 12 double-layer paper cases on baking trays.

2 Place the butter and sugar in a large bowl and beat together until light and fluffy, then gradually beat in the eggs. Fold in the grated carrots, walnuts, orange juice and rind. Sift in the flour and cinnamon and fold into the mixture until just combined. Spoon the mixture into the paper cases.

3 Bake the cupcakes in the preheated oven for 15–20 minutes, or until golden brown and firm to the touch. Transfer the cupcakes to a wire rack and leave to cool.

4 To make the frosting, place the cream cheese, icing sugar and orange juice in a bowl and beat together. Spread over the top of the cakes, then decorate with walnut halves.

VARIATION
To make 9-carrot gold cupcakes, use 85 g/3 oz grated carrot and 85 g/3 oz grated courgettes, and replace the walnuts with 55 g/2 oz sultanas. Decorate the top of each cake with a pecan nut.